UNCONDITIONAL HATRED

Books by Russell Grenfell:

THE ART OF THE ADMIRAL—*Faber & Faber*

THE MEN WHO DEFEND US—*Eyre & Spottiswoode*

SEA POWER—*Jonathan Cape and Doubleday*

THE BISMARCK EPISODE—*Faber & Faber and Macmillan*

NELSON THE SAILOR—*Faber & Faber and Macmillan*

MAIN FLEET TO SINGAPORE—*Faber & Faber and Macmillan*

UNCONDITIONAL HATRED—*Devin-Adair*

German War Guilt and the Future of Europe

Unconditional Hatred

CAPTAIN RUSSELL GRENFELL, R.N.

*We have grown accustomed to hear it insinuated that
all the adventures and anxieties and austerities of the
past half-century carried our country on until, in 1940,
it came to 'its finest hour'; and that may be, provided
it is stressed that what is meant is, not the finest hour
of the politicians who, if the truth be told, have shown
grievous ineptitude, bringing Britain to the very edge
of catastrophe by their imbecilities, but the finest hour
of the fighting men.*

(Algernon Cecil in QUEEN VICTORIA AND HER PRIME MINISTERS, p. 338)

THE DEVIN-ADAIR COMPANY   NEW YORK   1953

Many things can go wrong in war: minor tactics, major tactics, minor strategy, major strategy, supply, training, intelligence. Should there be failure in any of these, adverse consequences will ensue, to a greater or lesser degree according to the magnitude of the fault in relation to the war as a whole.

There is one other factor, however, in which error is nearly always serious. This is policy; since policy is the governing element controlling all the rest. The evidence regarding the Second World War indicates that American and British policy, both separately and in combination, suffered from defects of a major character. The greatest military effort in history was based on the belief that the complete defeat and permanent disarmament of Germany would exorcise the evil of war from the world. That belief turned out to be wholly false; so that in spite of all the bloodshed and sacrifice, Germany had to be asked to rearm shortly after the allied victory that was to mark the end of German military power. It is therefore clear that something was badly amiss with the approach to war of the American and British political leaders, and it is my purpose in this book to investigate and determine where they went wrong, with particular emphasis on the British aspect of the matter.

The reader will find that I have been somewhat iconoclastic. But I do not think it necessary to apologise for that. There is nothing, I fancy, in the handbook of democracy to suggest that politicians are immune from criticism. Surely very much the reverse. Freedom for the citizen to criticize his rulers is indeed the main distinguishing mark of a free society, and needs to be made use of if the power to do so is not to fall into decay.

Not that any sensible person would question the soundness of Winston Churchill's conduct of the war unless he felt, rightly or wrongly, that he had solid grounds for doing so; for captious criticism in that direction would harm only the critic.

Nor, I trust, am I insensitive to Sir Winston's truly remarkable qualities as a war leader. There was no other politician in Britain capable of infusing such enormous energy and resolution into the war effort as he. But that only makes it the more important to determine whether all his superabundant drive and vigour was being exerted in the right direction—or the wrong one. For Churchill's example is bound to have considerable influence on any of his successors who may find themselves in a similar position.

This book was completed just as Malenkov took over the reins of government in Russia, and electrified the world by his "new charm." I have, however, left the book substantially unaltered. Even if Russian policy is in process of drastic reorientation towards co-operation with the West, about which we cannot yet be certain, the problem presented by the military vacuum in central Europe would remain no less critical than in Stalin's time; possibly more so.

I am presented with a difficulty over Sir Winston Churchill's knighthood. It is from no discourtesy that I find it hard to bring all my references to the wartime Prime Minister up to date. It just doesn't sound right as applied to those days. One of the two or three most famous men in the world was for six hectic years thought of universally as "Mr." Churchill. It would in my judgment be doing violence to history to describe him otherwise in relation to those years. Besides, how am I to tell that by the time this book appears in print, Sir Winston Churchill may not be known by another title still?

I have received valuable help from a number of people in writing this book; to all of whom I wish to express my most grateful thanks. I prefer, however, not to make specific acknowledgment, as I wish to retain full and undivided responsibility for a book for which unqualified acclamation is hardly to be counted on.   R. G.

CONTENTS

UNCONDITIONAL HATRED

1

How Britain Entered the First World War

Twice in the lifetime of many persons now living, there has been a great "war to end war." It is true that neither war started quite like that, anyway as far as Britain was concerned. Indeed, of the various factors which led to British participation in the war of 1914, any idea of using violence to end violence finds no place. Britain entered the war for other reasons, and they are sufficiently intriguing to justify a brief examination as a prologue to the arguments which will be developed later in this book.

British embroilment in the war of 1914-18 may be said to date from January 1906, when Britain was in the throes of a General Election. Mr. Haldane, the Secretary of State for War, had gone to the constituency of Sir Edward Grey, the Foreign Secretary, to make an electioneering speech in his support. The two politicians went for a country drive together, during which Grey asked Haldane if he would initiate discussions between the British and French General staffs in preparation for the possibility of joint action in the event of a Continental war. Mr. Haldane agreed to do so. The million men who were later to be killed as a result of this rural conversation could not have been condemned to death in more haphazard a fashion. At this moment not even the Prime Minister, Sir Henry Campbell-Bannerman, let alone other members of the Cabinet, knew what was being arranged.

A few years earlier, at the turn of the Century, the British Foreign Office had made persistent efforts to conclude an alliance with Germany, but had been rebuffed. Disappointed in that direction, Britain had then turned towards Germany's rival, France, also a traditional rival of England's, and had effected a rapprochement with her. At this time, Europe was divided into two Power groups: the Triple Alliance of Germany, Austria, and Italy, and the Dual Alliance of France and Russia. By making friends with France, Britain was therefore making a gesture of sympathy towards the Franco-Russian group. But it was no more than a gesture, since when first made (in 1904) it consisted only of a settlement of outstanding points of friction between France and Britain, principally in Egypt and Morocco, France agreeing to give Britain a free hand in Egypt and vice versa as regards France in Morocco. Nothing was agreed about military assistance.

However, in the second week of January, 1906, when a new set of Ministers had just come into office in Britain, the French asked a question that was to have a dire influence on the course of British history. Their Ambassador enquired of Sir Edward Grey if conversations could be instituted between the respective Army Staffs to facilitate quick action should Britain come to France's assistance against a German attack. Any man of average intelligence and reasonable common sense might have been expected to realise the very tricky na-

ture of such conversations and to what a delicate and
even dangerous situation they might well lead. But apparently nothing of that kind occurred to Sir Edward
Grey. Hence his request to Mr. Haldane to get the
conversations under way even before anything had
been said to the Prime Minister. It is true that Mr.
Haldane agreed to mention the matter to the Prime
Minister before taking action, and did so; but no steps
were taken to consult the Cabinet about a proposal
that was supercharged with future possibilities of the
gravest kind. The matter remained for long a secret
with the three Ministers mentioned.*

Actually, there had already been—several months
before and under the previous Government—some
form of unofficial naval discussion. The French Naval
Attaché in London had asked the First Sea Lord (Sir
John Fisher) if the British wanted any French naval
help in the event of war, and had been told that, substantially, none was required. Hence, no British obligation towards the French was incurred in this way at
this period.

The three Ministers originally in the secret of the
military conversations agreed, and the French were
told, that nothing in any staff conversations must be
taken as committing Britain to positive action. But not
very much imagination was required to appreciate that
the conversations could not fail to be binding, and we
know from Sir Edward Grey's autobiography that they
came in the end to be as binding as a formal military
alliance, at all events as regards himself. Had the question been given full and leisured examination, it is
conceivable that the obvious pitfalls inherent in
the suggested conversations might have been appre-

---

* Lord Ripon, Government leader in the House of Lords, appears also to
have known, but took no active part in the matter.

hended in time. But they were hurried into operation by three—or really two—men during all the bustle and distractions of a General Election.*

So the talks began, and in five years' time resulted in the elaboration of very detailed and efficient plans to move six British Army Divisions to take their place on the left of the French line in twelve days from the commencement of mobilisation.†

These plans involved a drastic reshaping of higher army organisation, which had previously been devised for Colonial and not for Continental warfare. Mr. Haldane takes a good deal of credit to himself in his books‡ for this reorganisation, to which he is certainly entitled. But he is not entitled to the claim he also makes that it was due largely to "scientific thinking" on his part, both as regards the administrative reforms introduced and the strategy on which they were based. The reforms, as he himself admits, were not the consequence of deep and original thinking by him and his military advisers, either separately or in combination; they were mainly imitations of the German system which he deliberately and openly copied from information obtained during a visit to Berlin in 1906, though they were naturally adapted to British requirements. And, as we shall see, there was little that was scientific about the Haldane strategy.

This strategy was based on the belief that the six British Divisions which War Office calculations showed were the most that could be sent to France in

---

* Even as it was, the Prime Minister had serious misgivings. "I do not like," he said, "the stress laid upon joint preparations. It comes very close indeed to an honourable understanding." How right he proved to be.

† This was the plan as finally adopted. There had been variations in the earlier stages. See *Richard Burdon Haldane, An Autobiography,* Hodder & Stoughton, 1929, p. 188.

‡ *Before the War*—Cassell, 1920. Chapters VI & VII.

the first instance, were fortunately just the right number to redress the probable adverse balance of French
inferiority. It was a belief, however, which at least one
of Mr. Haldane's military advisers found too cautious.
Colonel Henry Wilson,* who in 1910 became Director
of Operations and therefore chief agent in succession
for the Haldane plan, by no means viewed the British
Expeditionary Force's task as that of preserving a
nicely calculated defensive balance. As his Diary shows,
his mental picture of a European war on the Haldane
model was that of a rapid series of glorious victories
by the Anglo-French Allies over the German enemy,
leading to the occupation of Berlin in a matter
of weeks. It is therefore hardly surprising that Wilson
threw himself heart and soul into the French military
conversations, in which he had indeed already managed to involve himself before going to the War Office.
He was a good French linguist and was frequently in
France cementing and extending his friendship with
members of the French General Staff, and pressing
steadily onwards with the plans for joint Anglo-
French military action.

By the middle of 1911, the arrangements for rapidly
transporting the British Army to the left of the
French line were more or less complete; and not till
then was it fully realised that there was serious dis-
agreement with the Haldane strategy from the opposite side of Whitehall. True, there had been muffled
rumblings of discontent from the Admiralty for a year
or two, the First Sea Lord (Sir John Fisher) being
fundamentally and openly hostile to the whole idea
of "Continental warfare," as his contemporary letters
to Lord Esher make plain.† For instance, he declared

* Later Field-Marshal Sir Henry Wilson.
† See Lord Fisher's *Memories*, pp. 206, 211.

in 1909 that "the dispatch of British troops to the front in a Continental war would be an act of suicidal idiocy arising from the distorted view of war produced by Mr. Haldane's speeches"; while even in 1912, after he had left the Admiralty, he was "fully agreeing" that "the schemes of the General Staff of the British Army (to support the French) are grotesque."

Fisher's own conception of the right use of the army was as a striking force employed in close conjunction with superior seapower for landings against the enemy's flank or rear. His vivid imagination visualised "the d—d uncertainty (on the enemy's part) of *when* and *where* a hundred thousand troops embarked in transports and kept 'in the air' might land," and he quotes a German General (Schwartzhoff) as saying that an army so utilised could be a "weapon of enormous influence and capable of deadly blows." This was in 1899 before the Anglo-French *entente*, and both Fisher and Schwartzhoff were thinking of war between Britain and France, then quite likely.*

Yet, in spite of Fisher's periodic fulminations against the Haldane strategy, it does not seem to have been until the Agadir crisis of 1911 that Grey, Haldane, and the Prime Minister (by then Mr. Asquith) came to realise that the very essence of the Haldane strategy was disputed by the Admiralty. Lord Haldane gives the impression in his *Before the War* that the Committee of Imperial Defence was an effective instrument in "co-ordinating naval and military war objectives" from 1905 onwards. This, however, is misleading to the point of being untrue. Sir John Fisher's anxiety was to "keep clear" of the Committee. In 1908, Fisher told Lord Esher that he was refusing to convey

---

* *Memories*, p. 212.

the naval war plan to anyone, even the Prime Minister; and in the following year he disclosed that Admiral Sir Arthur Wilson (who succeeded him as First Sea Lord) had told the Committee he refused to reveal the naval war plan, which was known only to him and Fisher!*

The imminence of war over the Agadir incident of 1911 forced Admiral Wilson's hand, and he informed the Committee of Imperial Defence that the Navy planned to land the Army in the Baltic immediately north of Berlin. Mr. Haldane and the General Staff were aghast. They had been labouring for years to perfect the arrangements for sending the British Army to France for the direct support of the French, and they naturally revolted against the prospect of these labours being rendered useless at the instance of ignorant naval officers. Furthermore, how could they have explained away such a strategical volte-face to the French Generals with whom they had by now established very close bonds of frequent consultation, professional sympathy, and personal friendship? It was unthinkable.

The naval ideas were immediately assailed by the War Office spokesmen. In his autobiography, Lord Haldane records with approval that one General sarcastically declared that even supposing the Army could be got to the Baltic, it would be "promptly surrounded by five or ten times the number of enemy troops." 'Promptly' was a questionable adverb to be used in this context, since the Germans would presumably not have known beforehand where the British were about to land, and so would not have had opposing forces in great superiority on the spot. The

* Lord Fisher, *Memories*, p. 194.

British invaders must therefore have had some time at least to make their presence felt.*

But whether German anti-invasion troops were ready waiting or whether they were brought from somewhere else, they could only have been provided at the expense of other areas; namely, the French and Russian fronts. The striking strength of the British Expeditionary Force as planned by Mr. Haldane and the British General Staff was six Divisions—actually one less than the first wave of the Normandy landing. If these six Divisions were to be "surrounded" by "ten times" their number of Germans, it means that sixty Divisions of Germans would have had to be found for the purpose. In 1914, there were initially about eleven German Divisions on the Russian front and eighty-three, including reserves, in the West. To remove sixty to the Baltic, either before or after a British landing, would thus have completely wrecked Germany's whole strategy, which would inevitably have been thrown into chaos. Had, therefore, the Admiralty plan of landing an army in the Baltic been feasible navally and been followed, and had the consequences been as the General Staff predicted, the British Baltic Army would undoubtedly have won the war in that hour. The British General Staff was, in fact, precisely endorsing Lord Fisher's estimate, made in the same year, that the Navy's Baltic plan would "demobilise about a million German soldiers."

But it is obvious enough that the General Staff spokesman had not thought the matter out. His argument was clearly the first thing that came into his mind for countering and discrediting the Admiralty's abominable idea. It is, however, somewhat odd that Lord

---

* It is doubtful if the Admiralty plan was practicable from the naval point of view, but the soldiers did not question it on these grounds.

Haldane should have set the argument down in cold print nine years later as proof of the Admiralty's stupidity, when a few pencilled calculations on the back of an envelope could have warned him he was on dangerous ground and that he was either enormously exaggerating the opposition a Baltic landing would have had to meet or greatly underestimating the diversionary effect of such a landing, and hence the relief it would have afforded to Britain's Allies. As it was, the force which went to France had no diversionary effect at all. Not a German Division was moved from its initial task. The British Expeditionary Force strengthened the Anglo-French armies by so many Divisions, but that was all.

And very distinctly all. The Haldane calculations had been falsified, as so often happens in war, by unforeseen factors; in this case, by the colossal blunders committed by the French General Staff, who made every mistake possible. They underestimated the German strength, they misjudged the likely enemy movements, they attacked in the wrong place themselves, and, owing to a blind adherence to a theory pushed to extremes, they pressed ill-advised offensives to the point of French annihilation. Instead of the British Army closing the expected gap in the line, as Haldane says was its intended function, it found itself engulfed by and swept along in the great French retreat to the Marne. It is, in fact, clear that, so far as the word "scientific" is applicable to strategy at all, the Admiralty's amphibious conception of the best use of an Expeditionary Force had much more science in it than Mr. Haldane's, even if the Admirals had underestimated the naval dangers of the Baltic project. The landing of the whole Expeditionary Force in Belgium after the German right wing had passed, and hence behind the

German front, would have been much more effective in dislocating the German plan and therefore in helping both the French and the Belgians, than a junction with the French Army. Nor would anything have been lost if the French offensives had been successful instead of disastrous failures.

But an even more weighty accusation remains to be levelled at Mr. Haldane's "scientific" approach to war, consistently ridiculed by Lord Fisher. The basic assumption on which Haldane's whole outlook towards a European upheaval rested was itself false. This was that if the Germans were able to push the French back and occupy the Channel coast of France, Britain's security would be gravely and even fatally imperilled. Holding this view, Mr. Haldane could plausibly believe that it was essential to use the British Army to keep the Channel coast of France out of German hands. This was a view also held by Sir Edward Grey, the Foreign Secretary, which accounts—or which at least he advances his own post-war autobiography as accounting—for his ready acquiescence in the French request for military conversations and for his personal conviction that the British Army should go to France.

That men of the mental calibre of Cabinet Ministers, and more especially when laying claim to a scientific outlook, could possibly have harboured so peculiar an idea is another illustration of how extraordinarily difficult it seems to be for landsmen, however intelligent, to hold sound views about sea power. There was no historical evidence at this time to suggest that an enemy occupation of the opposite coast of the English Channel would be lethal or even particularly dangerous to Britain. How could this be thought true, when that coast had in fact been in the hands of England's hereditary enemy, France, for centuries past? If the presence of an enemy on the coast between the Low Countries and Brest spelt disaster to England, why had that disaster never come from the hands of Napoleon I or the French Jacobins or Louis XVI, XV, or XIV, all of whom had held the south shore of the Channel while at war with England? The "scientific" answer, which surely should have appealed to Mr. Haldane if not to Sir Edward Grey, is that if these earlier enemies could not use the south coast of the Channel to overthrow the English, there was no real reason why Kaiser William II's Germany should have done it.

And if not, what was the need, not merely for the dispatch of an Expeditionary Force to France or even to the Baltic, but to anywhere at all? If the Fleet could be relied upon to keep England safe from attack, as history showed it could, was it not therefore better, if there was any doubt about Britain's security, to strengthen the Fleet until that security was put beyond question, instead of indulging in the unpredictable cost in men and money of Continental warfare on land? For long years during the Napoleonic wars, England had been kept safe by this means. Why not again? These were scientific questions which Mr. Haldane and Sir Edward Grey might have asked themselves as preliminaries to coming to a decision about the French conversations. But such questions clearly never occurred to them. They jumped straight to a superficial assumption which happened to be wrong.

That the two Ministers made this fundamental error of strategy was not their fault. They were not trained for war. But the question arises why they did not seek the advice of those who had been. Admiral Fisher's letters to Lord Esher during this period show that he entirely discounted the likelihood of invasion in the face of superior sea power. Either, therefore, Grey and Haldane did not ask the department most concerned, the Admiralty, for its expert opinion on invasion, or else they chose to ignore it and to blunder forward in pursuit of their own amateur view.

To return, however, to the Committee of Imperial Defence. Having vigorously countered the Admiralty's idea of landing a force in the Baltic, Mr. Haldane proceeded to carry the war into the enemy's camp. He declared that the Admiralty's plans differed from those of the War Office precisely because there was no scientifically organized Naval War Staff, and he threatened to resign from the War Office unless such a Staff were immediately installed. The threat was successful. A Staff was declared necessary for the navy—as indeed was true, though not for the reasons Mr. Haldane gave—and Mr. Churchill was sent to the Admiralty to see that the Sea Lords gave no more trouble to the War Office and its plans for Continental warfare on the grand scale. Thus it was that Britain came to pour her manhood out onto the European battlefields between 1914 and 1918 in support of pseudo-scientific arguments which were, in fact, quite bogus.

Almost more remarkable was the dramatic intervention in the Agadir crisis by Mr. Lloyd George with a speech conveying a clear threat of war to Germany. Most Britons at that time took it for granted that Mr. Lloyd George was the chosen mouthpiece of carefully weighed Government policy. We now know, however, that he was nothing of the kind. All by himself, in the recesses of the Treasury, Mr. Lloyd George had been undergoing a rising blood pressure at the contemplation of the German attempts to uphold their own interests against the evidence of French intention to seize Morocco. As a bargaining counter, the Germans had sent a gunboat to the Moroccan port of Agadir. This was too much for Mr. Lloyd George, the Chancellor of the Exchequer. Knowing nothing of strategy and without asking any expert's opinion, he made up his mind to utter a challenge to Germany in a speech he was due to make. *Only on the morning of the day he was to deliver the speech* did he mention his intention to a colleague, Mr. Churchill, then Home Secretary. He told the latter that he would speak about it also to the Prime Minister and the Foreign Secretary *after* that day's Cabinet. The First Lord of the Admiralty and the Secretary of State for War, who would have to deal with the war that Mr. Lloyd George's speech might well provoke, were apparently not considered worth consulting.

The speech was duly made and created the world sensation that might have been expected.* The chances of war were greatly increased, as the author has cause vividly to remember in consequence of the armoured cruiser in which he was then serving being suddenly ordered to return at full speed to the Fleet Base. Mr. Churchill records that he, the Foreign Secretary and the Prime Minister were "greatly relieved." Why they should have been is not at all clear. One would have thought that Grey, in particular, would not have relished his job being filched at a moment's notice by a fellow Minister who had neither the title nor the knowledge for handling foreign affairs or for precipitating a strategical crisis of the utmost gravity.

So we come to 1914 and the final eruption, when we are presented with another strange phenomenon. We have seen how Sir Edward Grey (still, in 1914, Foreign Secretary) and Mr. Haldane (by 1914, Lord Haldane and Lord Chancellor) came to the wrong con-

---

* Reported in *The (London) Times* of July 22, 1911.

clusions about the necessity for waging war against
Germany and, for the wrong reasons, made close and
elaborate preparatory arrangements with the French
for the dispatch of the Expeditionary Force to France.
To the last, Sir Edward Grey pretended to Parliament
that there were no such arrangements and that
Britain had an entirely free hand to enter a European
war or not.

It was an outrageous piece of deception. The
French had been led to suppose by repeated semi-
assurances and diplomatic encouragements that, in the
event of war with Germany, a British Army of a certain size would arrive in a certain area by a certain time
to fight with them, and they had come to count on its
arrival, disclaimers of "no commitment" notwithstanding. Had the Army not gone, there is little doubt
that they would have considered and proclaimed
themselves as basely betrayed, the written proviso
that Britain was not committed by the Anglo-French
military staff conversations being regarded as a "scrap
of paper." It was certainly so regarded by the British
Lord Chancellor and Foreign Secretary. The former
has put it on record that in his opinion British honour
required that Britain should go immediately to the
support of France,* while the latter has written that,
had she not, he himself would have felt compelled to
resign.† The resignation of the British Foreign Secretary immediately after the outbreak of war and because his country had not entered that war would have
been a step of the utmost political gravity which could
and undoubtedly would have done incalculable
harm to his country's interests and reputation. That
Sir Edward Grey, by his own admission, contemplated

* *Before the War*, p. 80.

† *Twenty-five Years*, Vol. 1, p. 312.

such a step makes palpable and sinister nonsense of his assurance to the House of Commons on August 3 that Britain was quite free and uncommitted as regards the war. If British honour demanded that Britain should support France against Germany, as both the Lord Chancellor and the Foreign Secretary agreed was the case, the latter's own honour required that he should say as much to the House of Commons. But he did not do so.

The fact is that Sir Edward Grey, by authorising those secret military conversations in 1906, had put himself into a position that he was now finding extremely awkward in 1914. If he told the House that the country was in honour bound to support the French in consequence of the conversations, the House would naturally have wanted to know why it had been kept in ignorance of these all-important negotiations which were dragging Britain into war. The alternative was to tell the House of Commons that Britain was in no way committed to war, a statement that Sir Edward Grey knew to be untrue. Sir Edward chose the path of untruth.

The average reader will note with interest that the British Foreign Secretary had felt himself entitled to assume personal obligations to a foreign Power independently of and in some respects contrary to the interests of his own Government and country: also that he would have resigned rather than be held to fail in his foreign obligations. On the other hand, he viewed a deliberately false statement to his own Parliament as quite compatible with continuance in office.

Sir Edward Grey, like most men who are not quite happy about their actions, has tried to justify his conduct. In his post-war book *Twenty-five Years*, he has chronicled at some length his reasons for believing

that Britain must in any event have entered the war
and at once. These reasons, which are to be found in
Chapter XVIII of his book, make up a highly instructive example of "fearful" thinking. Sir Edward first
indulges in a flight of imagination as to what would
have happened if the British Expeditionary Force
had not gone to France. Paris, he says, would have
been taken, France would have fallen, "huge defeats"
of the Russian, Army would have followed, Russia
would have made peace, and Germany would have
been supreme on the Continent.

What would have been Britain's position then? Sir
Edward answers this question as follows:

"We should have had no friend in the world; no one would
have hoped or feared anything from us or thought our
friendship worth having. We should have been discredited,
should have been held to have played an inglorious and
ignoble part. *Even in the United States we should have
suffered in good opinion.*"*

The outcome the reader can guess. We, in turn,
should have been attacked and overwhelmed.

Conjecture of this kind is irrefutable, because it
is the fanciful fruit of the untested past. The tested
past did not, however, support the gloomy imaginings
to which Sir Edward Grey thus gave full rein.
Napoleon I had managed to defeat all Continental rivals and dominate Europe. Yet he was not able
to overcome the obstacle of the English Channel
and deal with England as he dealt with Prussia,
Austria, and Russia. His "Army of England" lay en-
camped for many months at Boulogne, but could get
no further.

Nor had Britain been hated, despised, and thought

* *Twenty-five Years,* p. 36 (italics mine).

of no account because she had not sent troops to save
Austria from Austerlitz or Prussia from Jena. On the
contrary, she became the focus of hope for all those
who longed for delivery from Napoleonic domination.

Admittedly, Sir Edward Grey argued that the conditions of 1914 were quite different from those of 1805.
But he was wrong. For the even more different conditions of 1939-45 showed the old principles once
more coming into play. Hitler was no more able
to destroy an isolated Britain than Napoleon had been.
As for being hated and all that, the United States kept
out of both world wars as long as she could. Was she
publicly derided, despised and spurned for so doing?
The unctuous flattery that has flowed from Britain
towards America since 1939 gives the answer to that.
In this world, Governments do not pay tribute to virtue in other Governments but to power, as an experienced Foreign Secretary like Sir Edward Grey ought
to have known. Unfortunately, instead of shaping his
policy by what was best for his country, he had clearly
allowed his mind to become obsessed by pathological
visions of what other nations might think of the British—and perhaps of himself. The implications of his
apologia are that Britain must, for honour, for
safety, for self-preservation, plunge automatically into
any large-scale war that comes along: a suicidal thesis.
But, on Sir Edward Grey's own showing, it was this
thesis that took us into the 1914-18 war.

If Sir Edward Grey learnt nothing from that national catastrophe, one of his chief lieutenants did. No
one had been more active in support of the Grey-Hal-
dane pro-French policy than Colonel Henry Wilson.
As already mentioned, he did not regard the prospective dispatch of the British Expeditionary Force to

France as a means of avoiding the defeat of France by a narrow margin, as Grey and Haldane claim to have been their conviction, but as a glorious military adventure that was to lead the Anglo-French Allies into the heart of Germany before Christmas had come. Indeed, on August 1, 1914, Wilson was found in tears in the Admiralty building, in baffled rage at the seeming possibility that the British Army might not, after all, be allowed to enter the fight.

The four bitter years of war that actually ensued, where he had looked for perhaps four months, and the three million British and Imperial casualties changed Henry Wilson's view of Continental warfare and of his country's participation therein. "Next time," he told the officers of the Senior Officers School in 1920, when he was lecturing there as a Field-Marshal and Chief of the Imperial General Staff, "next time we must keep out of the scrum and pinch the mufflers."* Sound advice; but when the next time came, the example that Wilson had done so much to set on the former occasion proved too strong and carried all before it.

If Britain went to war in 1914 in defence of her honour and to avoid a miserable and ignoble future,† honour did not long retain its place on the headlines after the war had got fully into its terrible stride. By 1917, the people of Britain, France and the United States were being assured by their political leaders that the unprecedentedly dreadful conditions under which the great armies were having to fight would not be repeated, that Germany was responsible

---

* I am indebted to the late Lieut.-Colonel P. Villiers-Stuart for this information. Wilson was, of course, referring to spectators at a rugby match making off with the players' unguarded clothing.

† *Twenty-five Years*, Vol. II, p. 15.

for the war, and that when she was beaten steps could be taken and would be taken to create a new world in which war would be impossible.

In due course, the victorious Allies took the steps they judged necessary for this purpose. German armaments were ordered to be drastically reduced, to include a total prohibition of dreadnought battleships, submarines, tanks, and military aircraft. At the same time, the German colonies were taken away and, by the dismemberment of Austria, a number of succession states were created in Europe which, being in permanent alliance with France, presented Germany with a nearly complete ring of hostile bayonets. In addition, there arose a great new organisation called the League of Nations, which was to reinforce old-fashioned treaty combinations with the paramount safeguard of "collective security."

But even this combination of repressive measures did not prove effective in keeping Germany chained and impotent. By 1937 she had succeeded in casting off all restrictions and was once again mistress of her own fate.

The Second World War began, on Britain's part, in an even less intelligent way than the First. Sir Edward Grey and Mr. Haldane, whatever may be thought of their strategical intuitions, were at least planning to meet dangers that might arise close at hand. No one, however, can say that the issue that took Britain into the Second World War represented any danger to her at all. With extraordinary imprudence, the British Government had allowed itself to become involved in the German dispute with Czechoslovakia, a dispute with which it had no real concern, and in which it burnt its fingers very badly. Smarting under the ensuing criticism, it committed the further blunder in

the following year of letting itself be pushed by interested clamour into making a gesture to "stop Hitler"
by giving a guarantee to Poland against Germany. By
no possible stretch of argument could it be maintained that British security was in the least affected
by anything that might happen to Poland; while, if
British honour could be held to be involved, by virtue
of Britain being a signatory of the Treaty of Versailles
which had recreated Poland as an independent State,
the United States was equally concerned, as were also
France, Italy, and Japan. Moreover, a British guarantee of Poland against Germany was about as capable
of implementation as a guarantee of Mexico against
the United States. Hitler naturally knew this and declined to be deterred by such palpable bluff, and
Britain was driven into declaring war. The Second
World War thus began when the British Government
gave unyielding support to Polish retention of the
Polish Corridor. This had been a territorial device of
the Versailles peace-makers which for the next twenty
years intelligent people in Britain and elsewhere had
condemned as an impossible political arrangement,
in defence of which it was unthinkable that the British nation should ever be drawn into hostilities. Now
the unthinkable had come to pass.

But, once again, the struggle soon developed into
a crusade to end war. For the second time, Germany
was thunderously denounced as the trouble-maker,
and the anti-German world was assured that this
time there would be no half-measures. Germany's
power to plunge the planet into war would be broken
for ever, after which everyone would live happily ever
after.

Alas, it has not happened. Germany was duly
smashed in 1945, more thoroughly than any other

great warrior nation in a thousand years. But the mil-
lennium has not come. Very far from it. The world was
for the first eight years after the great smash in as bad
a state as at any time this century. Two great power
blocs were snarling at and openly arming against each
other, and the best the high politicians were able to tell
their publics was that they refused to believe that war
was inevitable, a slogan about as cheering as the rattle
of a spectre's chains.* And several lesser wars have
taken place or are in progress at this moment, including the gnashing of the United Nations' teeth in Korea.
Not only that, but Germany, whose total disarmament
was to be the grand solution to the world's ills, is being
begged to re-arm.

There is, as I think the reader will agree, something
wrong somewhere. The leaders of the victorious powers who had the fashioning of the future during the
latter part of the war, or some of these leaders, must
have gravely miscalculated and followed the path of
fallacy rather than wisdom. It is of great importance
to the rest of us to discover who it was that went wrong
and in what way.

---

* The true significance of Russia's new policy since Stalin's death remains
obscure.

2

Lord Vansittart and the German Butcher-Bird

When someone is ill and does not respond to the treatment prescribed, either the treatment may be wrong or the diagnosis of the malady. It is quite possible for a wrong treatment to be given for a right diagnosis. But if the diagnosis be wrong, the treatment is almost certain to be wrong with it. In re-examining the patient, it is therefore more sensible to begin with the diagnosis. I propose to apply this principle to the European problem.

First, I will take the "symptoms" relating to Germany's war guilt. The bulk of the British people believe that Germany started the last two world wars, and have good reason to believe it. They were told so repeatedly by Mr. Churchill during his wartime Premiership; and his statements to this effect have been supported on innumerable occasions by other politicians, by lawyers, church dignitaries, editors, and letter-writers to the Press. History is not the average Briton's strong point. Indeed, of warlike history he

is almost entirely ignorant, the teachers in our national schools having a prejudice against it. Hence,
the man in the street has had next to no reason to
doubt that Germany was the sole aggressor both in
1914 and 1939.

But the masses have been led to believe more than
that. They were subjected during the war to intense
and officially approved propaganda to the effect that
Germany has been the master trouble-maker throughout recorded history. Of this propaganda, one of the
most important examples was Lord Vansittart's *Black
Record,* a pamphlet which appeared in 1941 and went
into four impressions in its first two months. *Black
Record* was not the fervent outpouring of an ardent
patriot more enthusiastically anti-German than historically knowledgeable. It was written by a career
diplomat who was holding the highest post then available in the British Foreign Service; that of Chief
Diplomatic Adviser to His Majesty's Government.
A trained diplomat is supposed to have a sound working knowledge of the history of foreign countries, the
more important foreign countries especially. Lord
Vansittart's pamphlet consequently went out with a
prima facie hall-mark of complete accuracy stamped
on it. Actually, the influence on the public mind of
the pamphlet's message must have gone far beyond
its many thousands of readers. For the pamphlet itself was a recapitulation in print of a series of broadcasts previously given by the author, so that his views
must have reached millions of people.

For the following reasons it can be stated without
fear of contradiction that the Government, whether
or not they inspired Lord Vansittart's broadcasts and
pamphlet, did not disapprove of them: As a serving
official, Lord Vansittart (or rather Sir Robert Van-

sittart, as he was at the time) was forbidden by the regulations to make public any matter without the permission of his departmental superior, in this case the Foreign Secretary. Nor is it conceivable that a man of his high position and distinction would have dreamt of taking such a step, regulations or no, without assuring himself of Cabinet approval. But if, by some mischance or misunderstanding, the broadcasts, when begun, had proved distasteful to the chief Ministers of the Crown, we can be quite sure that a diplomatic illness would have overtaken Sir Robert Vansittart to prevent the completion of the series. It is therefore a reasonable assumption that what Sir Robert Vansittart said, His Majesty's Government thoroughly approved. Hence, the pamphlet is worthy of close study as showing what the inhabitants of the United Kingdom were encouraged to believe during the war, and what millions of them did believe and do to this day.

Lord Vansittart's main theme was simple. It was that Germany had been the constant and sole international trouble-maker from the beginnings of European history onwards; the one and only warmonger in a world otherwise inhabited by honest, trustful, peace-loving dupes of the German aggressor. The pattern had never altered. The Germans had always been the breakers of the peace; the rest of the world invariably the innocent and unsuspecting victims of German trickery and villainy.

Lord Vansittart, who is an excellent journalist, led off with a graphic illustration of this theme in his first chapter (and broadcast). He said that he happened to be at sea in a German ship in the Black Sea in 1907, when he noticed that the rigging was full of birds of different kinds being carried peacefully along with

the ship. Or so he thought at first. But soon he discovered that the birds had among them one seriously
malignant element which was completely ruining the
harmony. This was a shrike or butcher-bird, fierce,
heavy-beaked, murderous. One after another, it was
attacking and killing its fellow-travellers, the single
aggressor in the feathered company, the one gangster-
slayer.

Lord Vansittart went on to say that the conduct of
this butcher-bird immediately reminded him of Germany; for was not Germany, he thought to himself,
the butcher-bird of the nations? Was she not, just
like the shrike, the arch destroyer of international
concord by unprovoked, predatory, and homicidal
attacks? And had she not ever held this unique and
hateful position? He knew she had.

This was the argument that Lord Vansittart developed over and over again in six broadcasts and six
chapters of pamphlet. Germany was the butcher-bird
of the world. Germany was the brutal destroyer of the
peace. Germany was the international criminal; bloodthirsty, treacherous, and shameless. Here are three
examples of Lord Vansittart's theme and of the style
in which it was set forth. Thus:

On page 2: "Well, by hook and by crook—especially crook
—the butcher-bird got three wars before 1914 . . .
(each war) carefully planned and provoked by the
butcher-bird."

On page 16: "Hitler is no accident. He is the natural and
continuous product of a breed which from the dawn
of history has been predatory, and bellicose."

and on page 21: "Charlemagne had the lust for world-
domination so he had a war every year. . . . Eight
hundred years have passed, but in this respect the
German instinct remained constant."

Typical also of Lord Vansittart's summing-up of the German character is a statement on page 39 that:

"Germans have pledged no word without breaking it, have made no treaty without dishonouring it, touched no international faith without soiling it."

As a matter of fact, there is at least one exception to that sweeping condemnation which it is incumbent on the British, if no one else, to acknowledge. When the old Prussian Marshal Blücher was taking his army by forced marches towards the field of Waterloo, where the decisive battle with Napoleon was already in progress, he kept urging on his tired and hungry troops with the words, "I have given my promise to Wellington, and you would not have me break my word."

I cannot tell what motive Lord Vansittart had in writing (and speaking) about Germany in this strain. Whatever it was, his general historical argument about her was open to serious question. If the Germans had really been vile "butcher-birds" from the days of the Roman Empire onwards, the English had shown a frequent unawareness of that historical phenomenon. A hundred and thirty years before Lord Vansittart's *Black Record* appeared, they were saying just the same ugly things about a foreign nation; but not the Germans that time. In the first years of the nineteenth century, it was the French who were the "pests of the human race," in relation to whom no accusation was too bad and no language too strong. So it had been all through the eighteenth century, during the whole course of which our chief enemy in every European war had been France, whom we had fought in the reigns of Louis XIV, Louis XV, and Louis XVI; and, after the latter's execution, under the

Revolutionary Juntas and Napoleon. The young Nelson, growing up in the 1760s, learnt at his mother's knee that she "hated the French," and proceeded to hate them himself to the day of his death in 1805. This sentiment, widespread among the English, did not subside with the final defeat of Napoleon. Throughout the nineteenth century, France continued to be regarded as England's "hereditary enemy" and principal danger; and when plans for countering invasion were under consideration in London, it was always a French invasion that was in mind. Even the author, who is younger than Lord Vansittart, can remember being told in his boyhood about the French as the hereditary enemy.

Nor was Germany even the runner-up to France in popular antipathy. In the last quarter of the nineteenth century, a certain and subsequently rather famous refrain was a music-hall favourite in England, which went as follows:

> "We don't want to fight,
> But by Jingo, if we do,
> We've got the ships—
> We've got the men—
> We've got the money, too."

Who was it that we had the ships, the men, and the money to fight? The Germans? Not at all. The last three lines of the refrain went:

> "We have fought the bear before,
> We can fight the bear again,
> For the Russians shall not have Constantinople."

Against whom did Britain conclude the Anglo-Japanese Alliance of 1902? Against the Germans? Not so. Once more, it was against the Russians.

The mental connection that the young Vansittart formed between the butcher-bird and the German nation on that Black Sea trip in 1907 was, indeed, a very extraordinary one. For at that date, the Prussians were the only important European people against whom his country *had never fought*, whereas it had fought beside them on several occasions, notably the Seven Years' War of 1756-1763, and the wars against Revolutionary and Napoleonic France. In the campaign of the Hundred Days in 1815, the mainstays of the alliance that eventually overthrew Napoleon at Waterloo were the British and the Prussians, and one of the best-known pictures in military messes and clubs is that of Wellington and Blücher shaking hands on the field of battle.

If the Prussians were the butcher-birds of history, what were the British doing aiding and abetting them by fighting alongside them, and by granting them large subsidies to prosecute their own wars? To consort with and act as partners to international criminals was surely criminal conduct itself. Yet, somehow, we did not think of it like that in those days. Far from regarding the Germans as "butcher-birds," we were only too glad to have them at our side. Indeed, the Elder Pitt used to say that he had conquered Canada in Germany; another way of saying that the British Empire was built up on the German Alliance.

Nor was it only at our side that we British were happy to have German soldiers; we welcomed them in our ranks as well. In 1759, German troops to the number of 55,000 were taken into British pay. In the War of American Independence, Lord Howe's Army was largely composed of Hessians and Hanoverians; and at Waterloo Wellington's army contained nearly as many German troops as British, in the proportion of 19,700 to 23,900. If there was any merit in the overthrow of Napoleon on that occasion, Britain unquestionably owes no small degree of gratitude to those Germans, and to Blücher's 120,000 men for their help in bringing it about.

Lord Vansittart expresses no such sentiment. But perhaps his argument is that the Germans were only fighting the French because they could not get on for long without fighting somebody. This is the implication of his remark on page 29 that every time "you give the butcher-bird another chance, *he* will give *you* another war."

On this assumption, we ought to find that the Germans were the first to break the general peace that came to Europe with the final fall of Napoleon in 1815. Do we find this? Well, let us examine the facts.

1815-29

1823   A French Army crosses into Spain to support the King of Spain against his parliament.

1826   Russia goes to war with Persia and annexes two Persian provinces.

1827   A combined Anglo-French-Russian fleet attacks a Turko-Egyptian fleet at Navarino and destroys it.

1828   Russia invades Turkey in support of the Greek insurgents.

1830-39

1830   France commences the conquest of Algeria, which is not completed until 1847.

1831   The rebellion of Mehemet Ali of Egypt against Turkey brings in Russia against Mehemet Ali.

1839   Britain attacks Afghanistan (a failure).

1840-49

1840   The "Opium War" by Britain against China.
       British occupation of New Zealand, resulting in
       years of warfare against the Maoris.
1848   Piedmont declares war on Austria.

1850-59

1854   Crimean War between Britain, France, Pied-
       mont, and Turkey, on the one side, and Russia
       on the other.
1856   Britain goes to war with Persia.
1857   Britain begins a new war against China.
       Indian Mutiny against Britain.
1858   France (initially assisted by Spain) begins the
       conquest of Indo-China, which is not ended
       until 1863.
1859   Austria declares war on Piedmont, and France
       on Austria.
       The Anglo-Chinese war having been interrupted
       by the Indian Mutiny, it is now reopened, with
       the French helping the British, resulting in the
       sack and destruction of the Summer Palace, near
       Peking.

1860-63

1862   French expedition to Mexico, initially sup-
       ported by England and Spain.

Thus, in the first 48 years after Waterloo, we find
the British involved in six foreign wars, one Colonial
conquest, and the suppression of one major mutiny;
France involved in four foreign wars, and two Colonial
conquests: Russia involved in five foreign wars, without mentioning her eastern expansion in Asia and the
suppression of revolts in Poland (1830 and 1863) and

elsewhere; and Austria involved in two foreign wars, and the suppression of various revolts among the heterogeneous populations forming the Austrian Empire.

And what of the "butcher-bird" during this period, the butcher-bird of whom Lord Vansittart said in his pamphlet, "if you give him another chance, he will give you another war"? There were plenty of chances during these particular years. What advantage did the butcher-bird of Prussia take of them? The answer is, none at all.* Prussia was the only important State of Europe that remained at peace with her neighbours during all this long span of years, a near half-century of exemplary behaviour that no one else, including Britain, could show.

However, before one begins to think that Lord Vansittart may have confused butcher-birds with doves, it is necessary to go on a few years from 1863. And if we do that, we find Prussia breaking her peaceful record and indulging in three wars in the short space of six years. In 1864, she went to war with Denmark, in 1866 with Austria, and in 1870 with France. Yet even with these three, Prussia was not up to the post-Waterloo standard of Britain (6), France (5),* Russia (5), and no worse than Austria (3).† But were Prussia's three wars particularly bad examples of vicious, unprovoked attacks on unsuspecting neighbours? It is clear that Lord Vansittart thinks so, since he describes Prussia as having "crushed and plundered little Denmark," then bringing off a further "carefully contrived" war against Austria, and a similar war against France.‡ However, as our examination of the

---

* The temporary Prussian occupation of Schleswig-Holstein in 1848, which is dealt with in the next chapter, did not lead to hostilities.

* & † Including their respective wars with Prussia.

‡ *Black Record*, p. 24.

48 years after 1815 have hardly made Prussia look as wickedly aggressive as the oft-repeated epithet of butcher-bird would have led us to suppose, the cause of objective investigation calls for impartial scrutiny before accepting Lord Vansittart's verdict.

3

Germany and Denmark (1864) and Austria (1866)

Bismarck, says Lord Vansittart, was a "crafty Prussian bully" who, in 1864, "crushed and plundered little Denmark." * This reference to the Prussian-Danish War leaves us in no doubt about how we are expected to regard it—that it was a bare-faced and inexcusable piece of brigandage on the part of Bismarck's Prussia. A more detailed survey, however, of the Schleswig-Holstein question, the matter at issue between Prussia and Denmark at this time, invites a rather different conclusion.

To begin with, there was nothing new about the problem of the Duchies of Schleswig and Holstein. These were the border provinces between the Holy Roman Empire and Denmark, and like other border provinces they had for many centuries experienced troubled careers, while the numerous changes in their national allegiances, types of rulers, and relations to each other, as a result of wars, dynastic inheritances, and inter-State treaties, were extremely complicated.

* *Black Record*, p. 24.

However, certain broad features of the question of the Duchies as it stood in the middle of the nineteenth century can be stated. In the first place, the southern Duchy of Holstein was wholly German in population. The Schleswigers were rather more mixed, but a large proportion were German by blood and sentiment. Moreover, by ancient claim, not always admitted by Danish authority but never abandoned by the inhabitants, the two Duchies were held to be indissolubly linked together in semi-autonomous privilege.

One of the distinctive features of the nineteenth century was the emergence and growth of nationalism all over Europe. It was felt everywhere. Italians were longing to be freed from foreign yoke and to form a united country of their own. There was violent agitation among the Poles against their Russian and German overlords, while in the Balkans the subject races of the Turk were early planning and plotting to gain their independence.

It is not therefore surprising that the Germans of Schleswig and Holstein should begin to feel the urge for union with their kith and kin of Germany. Their first chance came in 1848, the year of revolution when disturbances broke out in every country of Europe. The King of Denmark invited trouble by trying to incorporate Schleswig into Denmark proper, thus attacking the traditional association of the two Duchies and also Schleswig's ancient position of separate identity. As a result, both Duchies broke out in revolt against the King's action, declared their independence, and demanded admittance into the German Confederation. Feeling in Germany was excitedly on the side of the Duchies, and Prussian troops marched in and were on the point of settling the affair in the way the local inhabitants wanted when other Powers intervened to preserve the status quo. Sweden landed an army and Britain sent a fleet to the Baltic, while Russia threatened similar action. Faced with this international opposition, Prussia withdrew; and the Duchies were left without support, though they remained adamant about their aspirations to join up with Germany.

At this point, it may help if a few words are said about the general organisation of central Europe, which at this time contained some complicated and confusing features, mainly relics of a past and discarded conception, the Holy Roman Empire.

This latter came into effective being in 800 A.D., when Charlemagne was crowned Roman Emperor of the West by Pope Leo III, though the title Holy Roman Empire dates from his successor, Otto I, of a century and a half later. Charlemagne's Empire comprised the northern half of Italy, France, Western Germany, and Austria. As time passed, there were modifications. Western France passed outside the Empire and the latter's eastern boundary tended to move eastward, until the Ottoman conquests made a north-westerly bulge in the Balkan area. In the Sixteenth Century, the Empire may be said to have extended from Rome on the south to the Baltic on the north, and on the west from the rough line Ostend-Nice to the borders of Poland and the Ottoman Empire on the east, the position of Hungary being a fluctuating one, sometimes in and sometimes out. On the whole, however, and though it included the Low Countries, Burgundy, Franche Comté, Savoy, and north Italy, the Empire was essentially a Germanic one and bore as its full title "the Holy Roman Empire of the German Nation."

But it was far from being a political unity, being made up of a large number of the Kingdoms, Principalities, Grand Duchies, Duchies, and Electorates, into which the modern Germany was then divided and sub-divided in bewildering multiplicity. Over this conglomeration of States, large and small, the Holy Roman Emperor did not rule. His position was rather that of an honorary patron than of an executive chairman. The many constituent states of the Empire did not want to be ruled. They wanted independence; if necessary, freedom to make war on each other. The Emperor did, however, stand as a focus of Teutonic sentiment and a sense of racial cohesion. The Empire had its Parliament or Diet, as it was called, which met from time to time. Its deliberations were, however, usually barren of practical results. It more or less resembled a modern dining club, the members of which, having similar interests, met periodically for a pleasant gossip and a convivial evening.

From the 13th Century, the office of Holy Roman Emperor was elective; but from the 16th Century until its end at the beginning of the 19th Century the Emperor was always a Hapsburg, ruling in Vienna; so that the Hapsburg dynasty, which lasted in Austria until the 20th Century, came to acquire all the prestige associated with what was, in fact, the hereditary position of Holy Roman Emperor, a prestige in which Vienna shared as the Empire's traditional capital.

The Holy Roman Empire was killed by the ferment of new ideas emanating from the French revolution combined with the dazzling victories of Napoleon. In 1806, the Emperor Francis II, fearing that the Corsican conqueror intended to usurp the ancient Imperial title himself, skilfully forestalled him by formally abandoning it and taking instead that of hereditary Emperor of Austria.

With the end of the Napoleonic upheaval in 1815,

it had to be decided how the Europe that had suffered such batterings and dislocations at the hands of
the Napoleonic armies was to be organised for the future. The Holy Roman Empire was dead, but much of
its accompanying tradition was still alive. The surviving Germanic States of central Europe, greatly reduced in number but correspondingly increased in size
by conquest or forcible amalgamation, did not revive
the structure of the old Empire yet did not disclaim
its basic ideas of racial unity and inter-State consultation; though without surrendering any real individual sovereignty. Austria and Prussia, the two chief
Germanic powers, were highly jealous of each other,
and the lesser States were jealous of both. Yet, in spite
of that, there was an undoubted feeling for some sort of
combination.

As a result, a Constitution for Germany emerged
from the Congress of Vienna. There was to be a Confederation of the German States (or Bund) for the
maintenance of the external and internal security of
all, each State agreeing to defend any of the others
against attack and engaging not to make war on other
member-States of the Confederation.

This league of the German peoples was almost as big
a sham as the larger League of Nations that came into
existence (for a time) in 1919. Lacking political unity,
the Confederation was no safeguard to its constituent
members, either collectively or singly; and individual
States did not hesitate to make war against each other
when it suited their purpose.

However, like the League of Nations, the Confederation looked well on paper and sounded even better in
oratorical perorations. It was given a central deliber-
ative body, the Federal Diet, which sat at Frankfort
under Austrian presidency. Theoretically, the Diet

could do a lot; practically, however, it was almost impotent. Nevertheless, the Confederation was still in existence when the Schleswig-Holstein question had arrived at a critical stage; to which question we can now conveniently return.

Everyone concerned, the Duchies, the Danes, and the Great Powers, was anxious for a quick solution, since it was known that the matter must come to a head when the King of Denmark, Frederick II, died. By Danish law, the royal succession could continue through the female line. But in the two Duchies, the opposite had been the traditional rule. And King Frederick had no male heir.

In 1852, a Conference of the major Powers assembled in London to seek a way of averting this prospective crisis, the Conference being attended by representatives of Austria and Prussia, but not of the German Confederation. The Conference, with Austrian and Prussian concurrence, decided that King Frederick's indirect heir should succeed to the Duchies. The Holsteiners at once challenged the validity of the award.

In 1862, a new King, William I, ascended the throne of Prussia and at once called one Otto von Bismarck to be his Chancellor. The next year King Frederick of Denmark died, and the new King, Christian IX, prepared to take over the Duchies in accordance with the London agreement of 1852. But the German Diet, for once doing something active, declared it was not a party to the 1852 agreement, and at its instance a Saxon and Hanoverian Army marched into Holstein in the name of the Confederation's candidate, the Prince of Augustenburg.

This move by the Diet was most fortunate for Bismarck. Before he had risen to power, his country

had put its signature to the 1852 agreement, but this
was a legacy not at all to his taste. Bismarck was a man
of long views and high ambition for his country's future; indeed, for the future of the whole German
people. In the Duchies of Schleswig and Holstein, he
had already visualised a naval base for a future German fleet in the magnificent harbour of Kiel, and a
deep-water canal through Schleswig which would give
the fleet easy access to the North Sea. For these aims to
become realities, he knew that Schleswig and Holstein
must become Prussian provinces.

One stumbling block was the 1852 treaty that
Prussia (and Austria) had signed. Though the action
of the Diet in sending troops into the Duchies offered
a way round that, Bismarck knew that Prussia could
not move by herself alone.What he succeeded, however, in doing was to induce Austria to move with her;
and the two strongest powers in Germany marched
in.

They were met by the Danes with armed opposition,
which was naturally foredoomed to failure. That the
Danes resisted at all was almost certainly due to their
confident belief that Britain would come to their aid.
Lord Palmerston had just previously made a speech in
Parliament which practically pledged British support
to the Danes, a speech which had been acclaimed with
enthusiasm by the British public who, knowing nothing at all of the rights and wrongs of the case and influenced by the fact that the Prince of Wales had only
recently married a Danish Princess of great personal
charm, looked ignorantly upon the Schleswig-Holstein
dispute as a simple instance of "small hero versus large
bully," and were typically incensed. But Palmerston
found he had miscalculated, and the Danes were left
to their fate. They were defeated in a very short time,

and the Duchies passed into the joint possession of Prussia and Austria.

We are now in a position to assess the validity of Lord Vansittart's accusation that Bismarck was a "crafty Prussian bully who crushed and plundered little Denmark." The first defect in this statement is that the implied accusation that Bismarck and Prussia were the only plunderers of Denmark (if plunderers there were) is untrue. Austria joined with Prussia in the Danish war.

The next question is whether the word "plundered" is appropriate at all. The territory "plundered" was not inhabited by Danes but, except for a small area in north Schleswig, almost exclusively by Germans who had for generations been hotly desirous of joining up with Germany; and the Austro-Prussian campaign to allow them to do so was but the application of that principle of self-determination about which the British (with their other allies) were so enthusiastic—at German and Austrian expense—at the Versailles Peace Settlement of 1919. And if Denmark was "crushed" in 1864 in a hopeless war against two main Germanic Powers, it was largely because Britain, having allowed Denmark to think that British help could be relied upon, backed out at the last moment and left her in the lurch.

So much for the Danish War. It left Prussia and Austria in joint possession of the Duchies; and, as might be expected, conflict of opinion between the two victors about what should be done with them soon began to manifest itself. The Austrians were for handing them over to Prince Augustenburg as a new Principality within the German Confederation. Bismarck, however, had other plans, though he did not yet disclose them. He wanted the Duchies, as has already been mentioned, for Prussia, as part of that larger project of a unified Germany under Prussian hegemony which was in his mind; and particularly for the provision of a main naval war base at Kiel and the cutting of a strategic canal between the Baltic and the North Sea. And if the acquisition for Prussia of these non-Prussian Duchies for such long-range strategic reasons be held to be evidence of wickedness on Bismarck's part, it may be useful to glance at the conduct of another country also interested in the construction of a deep-water canal.

At the turn of the 19th–20th Centuries, the United States of America was anxious to construct a commercial and strategic canal through the Isthmus of Panama. The area selected belonged to the Republic of Colombia. Negotiations were opened between the American and Colombian Governments regarding the necessary concession for the building of the canal. An offer was made to Colombia of $10,000,000, an annual rental of $250,000 when the canal was in being, and certain other benefits. The respective negotiators agreed to these terms, which were ratified by the United States Senate. Colombia, however, refused her consent, in the hope of forcing the terms up higher. A dramatic development then took place which strongly suggests that American politicians were not any less "crafty" than Otto von Bismarck of Prussia. A revolution broke out in the province of Panama, which declared its independence of Colombia. Colombian troops were despatched to deal with the revolt, and would probably have had no difficulty in doing so had not the American warships actively prevented their being landed; and four days after the outbreak, the United States Government recognised a new Republic of Panama, which immediately made over the canal strip to American sovereignty. And Colombia got nothing at all until many years had passed.

To return now to central Europe. Bismarck not only wanted the two Duchies: he intended also to unify the German peoples under one authority. This was an objective he had every justification for pursuing. The tessellated condition of Germany, split up into numerous small states and "free cities," had been a source of extreme weakness for centuries. This lack of cohesion and centralised control was the main reason why the European wars of the 17th and 18th Centuries were fought on German territory instead of that of Germany's enemies.

Moreover, the political unity and independence of kindred peoples was in the air. A little earlier, Cavour had been actively and openly working for the unification of Italy and, by the time of his death in 1861, he had already achieved a large measure of success. The Serbs, Bulgars, and Rumanians had been simmering with discontent against Turkish rule ever since the successful Greek revolt of the 1820s. The Poles had risen against Russia in 1863. And, in the new world of America, a fierce and bloody war for national unity had just been fought between the North and South. There was therefore nothing unusual about Bismarck's desire for German unity and greater strength. Britain, it may be remarked, had carried through her insular amalgamation in 1707 with the Union of England and Scotland, which greatly increased the security and considerably strengthened the power of the two countries in combination.

If, however, Germany were to be unified, there were, as Bismarck knew, two claimants to the leadership of the Union—Austria and Prussia. Austria had the immense advantage of being the legatee of the tradition of the not-long-defunct Holy Roman Empire. Vienna had been the acknowledged centre of the Germanic world for a thousand years. Prussia, on the other hand, was regarded in Germany as a rather vulgar *nouveau riche*. Bismarck, however, and apart from the fact that he was a Prussian, could reasonably argue that Prussia was the proper leader for a united Germany. Austria was mixed up with all sorts of non-German peoples comprising her Empire: Czechs and Slovaks in Bohemia, Serbs, Croats, and Slovenes on the Adriatic, Hungarians and Italians. If Austria took the leading position, the united German peoples would inevitably become involved in the problems, often tiresome and sometimes dangerous, of these subject races of the Austrian Emperor. Prussia, on the other hand, was almost entirely unencumbered in this way, her slice of Poland only excepted. German unity under Prussia would be truly German in character and interest.

But how was the other claimant, Austria, to be disposed of? Bismarck believed it could only be done by a trial of strength in war. Cavour had also relied on the primary sanction of armed force for the unification of Italy, and this not only in Italy itself. He had deliberately sent a contingent of Piedmontese troops to participate in the Crimean War against Russia, with whom he had no possible quarrel, in order that the Piedmontese ruling House of Savoy, which Cavour intended for the leadership of Italy, might increase its prestige and bargaining power with France and Britain. If war was a means to a political end with Bismarck, so it was with Cavour.

Both Austria and Prussia knew that the trial of

strength was coming and both prepared for it. Bismarck was aware that he had not only to deal with Austria but with the German Confederation. From this he did not shrink. At his instance, the Prussian Army had been reorganised by the soldiers, von Roon and von Moltke, and Bismarck believed it to be the best in Europe. But he wished to make assurance doubly sure. He bribed the Piedmontese with the promise of the Venetian province, then held by Austria, if they would come into the war on his side. He had gained the friendship of Russia by refusing to join with France in protesting against the brutal Russian methods employed in putting down the Polish insurrection of 1863; and, finally, he hinted to Napoleon III of pickings to be obtained after an Austro-Prussian war in which France remained neutral. Napoleon III indeed visualised himself as intervening with advantageous effect as mediator in the final stages of a struggle which would surely enfeeble both contestants.

Bismarck then, in 1866, found means of forcing the issue regarding Schleswig-Holstein, and Prussia declared war on Austria, Saxony, Hanover, Hesse, and the rest of the German Confederation. All was soon over. The Confederation was easily overcome. The Austrians proved a slightly tougher problem but their army was finally smashed at Königgrätz six weeks after the declaration of war.

Lord Vansittart says that this war was "carefully contrived" by Bismarck, and so it was; though had Austria won, the same could probably have been said about her. But, as an example of the work of the universal butcher-bird, who eats up other nations, this war could hardly be less impressive. Bismarck took nothing from Austria for himself. Except for the Venetia which he had promised to Italy, he left Austria intact.* Indeed, he went further than this. He restrained the King of Prussia from marching into Vienna and dictating peace from the beaten enemy's capital. It was no part of Bismarck's object to humiliate or unduly weaken Austria. That object was to destroy the lingering tradition of the Holy Roman Empire by pushing Austria outside Germany, to abolish the German Confederation in its then form, and to annex Schleswig-Holstein. On these Bismarck insisted; but, having gained them, he practised the utmost leniency towards the Austrian enemy.

As a first step towards German unity, Bismarck formed a new North German Confederation, which acknowledged Prussia as its head. He left the southern and Catholic States (Bavaria, Saxony, Württemburg, Baden—those nearest in sympathy with Austria) undisturbed. He meant to include them eventually in the greater Germany he was building up, but he felt that the time was not yet ripe.

* With the hostile States of the German Confederation he was, in furtherance of his unification policy, more severe; Hanover, Hesse-Cassel, Nassau, and Frankfort being annexed to Prussia.

4

The Butcher-Bird and France (1870)

And so we come to the Third Act of the six-year trilogy of Prussian "butchery" between 1864 and 1870. This time the victim was France, against whom another "equally well contrived" war was brought off by Bismarck, who had "gauged the weakness of the French Empire as Hitler had gauged the weakness of the French Republic."* But this war, the Franco-Prussian war, was also the first act of a new trilogy of conflict between France and Germany. One of the common sayings in post-1945 Britain frequently to be read in leading articles in and letters to the Press, relates to the repeated sufferings of innocent France, invaded and tortured by the brutal Germans thrice in seventy years. Therefore, many people declare, France has every right to adequate assurances of security against further wanton and unprovoked attacks by her turbulent and aggressive neighbour across the Rhine. After all, thrice in seventy years! It is too much.

It will be useful to keep this public attitude in mind

---

* *Black Record*, p. 24.

in examining the three wars between France and Germany of 1870, 1914, and 1939, the first-mentioned being our immediate subject.

No problem is usually less simple than the reasons which lead up to any war, a major war especially. These reasons hardly ever have their whole origin in contemporary events, but are more often a jumble of ancient causation and immediate crisis. Such was the case here. In 1870, the French still regarded themselves as the greatest nation of Europe. For two hundred years, France had been the leader of fashion, civilisation, and military achievement. She had, it is true, been defeated in 1814 and 1815, but only by a vast combination of powers leagued against her. And the ten previous years had been glorious with a record of victory and conquest under Napoleon I that had been unequalled in history. In 1870, another Emperor Napoleon was on the throne of France, and the glittering traditions of the *grande armée* of his illustrious uncle lived on in the dreams of the nephew. He and his generals believed the French army to be incomparable.

Nevertheless, Napoleon III could not view with composure the expansion of Prussian power as a result of the Austro-Prussian war. Like the English, the Germans were natural enemies of the French, and the consolidation of all north Germany under Prussian leadership was not a welcome development. Moreover, Napoleon III had been chagrined by the swift victory of Prussia over Austria in 1866. His anticipated mediation between two exhausted opponents and the territorial "compensation" he had hoped, under Bismarck's skilful encouragement, to extract as the price of his neutrality, had not materialised. Prussia, the victor, had not been exhausted and was turning a deaf ear to French suggestions for *douceurs*, to the grave annoyance of the French politicians and the sensible lowering of the domestic prestige of the French Emperor. In the course of the following few years, France kept putting in one claim after another—for bits of West Germany territory, for the Saar, for Luxemburg, even for Belgium. But Bismarck was agreeing to none of this, although he filed the French notes away with cheerful anticipation of their shortly being useful.

Bismarck had made up his mind that war with France was unavoidable. He had unified half Germany; but there was still the other half. South Germany was not yet inside the Prussian orbit, and Bismarck was determined to get it there. But he did not think that France would peacefully look on while German strength received this large accretion. Nor did he believe he would be able to attract the south German states into the Prussian fold without the stimulus of a foreign, and particularly a French, war to arouse their German patriotism.

And now Napoleon himself was to acquire an incentive for a war against a European enemy. In 1862, he had been imprudent enough to send an expedition to Mexico with a view to replacing the Republic in that country by an Empire over which Maximilian, brother of the Austrian Emperor, was to reign. The project was soon seen to be based on a grave miscalculation of local sentiment, and came to an ignominious end in 1867 after the United States of America, just emerged from the distractions of their Civil War, had bluntly ordered the French troops to withdraw. No sooner were they gone than the newly created Emperor Maximilian was taken prisoner by his enemies and shot.

The damage to French prestige, and correspondingly to Napoleon III's personal position, was tremendous;

and in this extremity he began to consider the possibility of restoring his political reputation by seeking
military glory through a European war. Or rather, some
of his advisers did. For Napoleon III himself was by
this time a sick man, suffering from a painful internal
complaint which had much affected his personal efficiency and resolution. But both the Empress and the
Foreign Minister, Gramont, were advocates of a war
policy. Both were confident of success in the event of
hostilities, for was not the French army of ancient re-
nown and of the highest efficiency? And had not the
Chief of the General Staff reported it as ready for war
'to the last gaiter button'? A conflict with Prussia
could therefore be contemplated with equanimity,
in anticipation of which negotiations were opened for
an alliance with Austria, Prussia's worsted opponent
of 1866.

Meanwhile, Bismarck was busy consolidating the
newly-created North German Confederation and laying his plans for the next move, a move which
he hoped would bring on war with France. In 1870,
he played a very cunning card. It was suddenly announced that a Prince of Hohenzollern, of the same
house as the rulers of Prussia, had accepted the vacant
throne of Spain. There is little doubt that Bismarck was
behind the Prince's candidature, which had two advantages. If it did not lead to war between Prussia and
France it might well result in war between France and
Spain, almost as useful from Bismarck's point of view.

No sooner was the candidature known than France
was in a ferment. Excited and bitter speeches were
made, and there was open talk of war. But just as vol-
atile French anger was reaching its climax, the situation was suddenly eased by the news that the Prince
had been induced to withdraw his candidature. The

French were jubilant; Bismarck was cast into gloom. As has been mentioned, however, there were war parties in each country, in France as well as in Germany, the first of which included the French Foreign Minister. Gramont now proceeded to take a step more than likely to precipitate a crisis. Not content with France's diplomatic triumph, he instructed the French Ambassador to Prussia, who was at Ems, where the Prussian King was also staying, to obtain from William I an assurance that he would not allow the Prince's candidature ever to be renewed. This insulting demand King William naturally refused, albeit without incivility; but he telegraphed an account of the episode to Bismarck in Berlin. Bismarck condensed this telegram into a shorter *communiqué* for the Press in such a way that, while the essential truth of the interview between the French Ambassador and the King of Prussia was preserved, the latter's refusal of the assurance sought was made to appear more blunt. But to call the condensation a "forgery," as Lord Vansittart does, is an absurd exaggeration.*

However, the Bismarck *communiqué* was enough to send the French kettle boiling over again. One section of the Cabinet, headed by Gramont and encouraged by the Empress, pressed for war. The Emperor and several Ministers were for peace. What really decided the issue were the inflammatory orators in the French Chamber and the clamour of the Parisian mob. The latter were for war. The streets resounded to shouts of *"à Berlin"* and *"vive la guerre."* The people's will carried the day. Early next morning France declared war on Prussia.

Had the people of Paris had any real knowledge of

---

* The texts of the King's telegram and Bismarck's communiqué are given in Appendix I.

the state of the French Army, they would have kept silent. As a warlike instrument, that army proved gravely inferior to the carefully organised, brilliantly staffed, and recently war-tried Army of Prussia. In a matter of weeks, the French were beaten time after time and at Sedan the Emperor Napoleon himself was taken prisoner.

The British did not intervene on the outbreak of war. Bismarck, with consummate timing, published Napoleon's previous proposal for France to be given Belgium. With their sensitiveness about the Low Countries, this was quite enough to swing the British to the Prussian side. A similar publication of Napoleon's request for a slice of West German territory also sufficed to rally South Germany behind Prussia; and in January, 1871, the establishment of the German Empire was proclaimed at Versailles Palace. Bismarck had achieved his great object of unifying the German peoples (outside Austria) in six short years, with the aid of three wars which altogether amounted to less than a year's fighting. When peace was made in 1871, Bismarck annexed the border provinces of Alsace and Lorraine, which had originally been German and whose inhabitants were of mixed German and French stock and speech.

Here, then, is the first of the three wars in which France was wickedly invaded or ravaged by the Prussian butcher-bird. It is, I think, sufficient to mention that it was France and not Prussia that declared war, that the war was highly popular with the common people of Paris, who expected that the French Army would march straight through to Berlin, as did most of the French Generals.* If, as Lord Vansittart says,

---

* Lord Bryce, in his *Holy Roman Empire*, expressed the opinion that the French appeared to be the aggressors. (p. 473)

Bismarck had gauged the weakness of the French Empire, the French had signally failed to gauge the strength of the Prussian military machine, and consequently paid the penalty for their ignorance about their rivals, and for their gross over-confidence about themselves. And for these French defects, neither Bismarck nor Prussia can be blamed. The Poles made much the same cardinal blunders about Hitler's Germany and the Polish Army in 1939.

The second Franco-German war and German invasion of France came, of course, in 1914. But before going on to consider that conflict, it will be useful to list the wars that took place between 1870 and 1914. Leaving out the relief of the Peking Legations, which was an international affair, the ordinary wars over this period were as follows: In 1877, Russia fought Turkey. In 1879, Britain went to war with the Zulus, and in 1882 with Egypt. In 1883 occurred the first war between Britain and the Boers of the Transvaal. In 1894, there was war between China and Japan and in 1898 between the United States and Spain. In 1899, the second war between Britain and the Boers—known generally as the South African War—broke out and lasted for three years. In 1904, Russia and Japan came to blows. In 1911, Italy went to war with Turkey; and in 1912 the Balkan countries of Serbia, Bulgaria, and Greece first attacked Turkey and then fell out among themselves.

What of our friend the "butcher-bird" during this troubled period? Strangely enough, we again find her preserving peace with her neighbours. Between 1870 and 1914, a matter of 44 years, the Germans engaged in no war with another Power, while Britain, Russia, Italy, Turkey, the Balkan States, the United States and Spain were all involved. Of the main Powers, only

Germany, Austria, and France had a clear record. The warlike score, therefore, from 1815 up to the year 1907 (when Robert Vansittart, observing the butcher-bird at work in the Black Sea, naturally thought of Germany), stands as follows:

Britain	10
Russia	7
France	5
Austria	3
Prussia-Germany	3

Let us now examine the origins of the 1914 war, remembering that we do so especially as regards the question of German guilt for that war and in particular as compared to France.

It has already been remarked that at the very end of the nineteenth century, Britain made advances for an alliance with Germany, which the latter rejected, whereupon Britain turned instead to France. In the years immediately preceding this Anglo-French rapprochement, the relations between the two countries had been bad to the point of danger. France had been highly jealous of Britain's position as the paramount power in Egypt, and in 1898 there had very nearly been war over the Fashoda incident in the Sudan. Britain, for her part, had been sourly suspicious of French ambitions in Morocco. The *entente* of 1904 resolved these rivalries, with consequences that we shall shortly examine.

In 1905, after the British and French had decided to adjust their differences, the international political situation of the European Powers was as follows. Central Europe was united in a Triple Alliance of Germany, Austria, and Italy. Neither Germany nor Austria had much faith in Italy's loyalty to the Alliance, and believed she would desert it if it suited her to do so. In this, they were right.

The other principal alliance was that between France and Russia, who were joined in an offensive-defensive pact to support each other in war. The war both contemplated was, of course, war with the Triple Alliance. The French had never allowed themselves to become reconciled to the loss of Alsace and Lorraine in 1871. Though these provinces had originally been German and had been acquired by France partly by force, the French were implacably determined to get them back and remained inflexibly hostile to Germany in consequence. The Franco-Russian alliance was a natural stepping-stone to the realisation of this aim. The Russians embraced the alliance for reasons of their own which we shall notice in a moment. After 1904, Britain inclined towards the Franco-Russian group, but did not specifically join it. Nevertheless, the term Triple Entente came into being to designate the association of Russia, France, and Britain in diplomatic accord.

The most serious causes of European friction in the ten years between the Anglo-French *entente* of 1904 and the outbreak of general war in 1914 were caused by the expansionist ambitions of two States: France in Morocco, and Serbia in the Balkans.

The Anglo-French *entente* included a secret agreement that France would leave Britain a free hand to dominate Egypt, in return for a free hand to do the same to Morocco. In public, of course, the Entente Powers did not admit to this. Indeed, they declared they were united in their determination to preserve Moroccan independence, but their true determination was just the contrary.

The French were not slow in taking advantage of

British connivance in their Moroccan plans, and they set on foot the preliminary moves that were meant to lead eventually to a French protectorate over the Sultan of Morocco's territory. Unfortunately for the smooth realisation of the plan, the Germans soon began to suspect what was afoot. Six or seven years before, when Britain had been more friendly disposed towards Germany than towards France, the British Foreign Office, then hostile to French expansion in Morocco, had invited Germany to seize various ports, including Casablanca, on the Moroccan Atlantic coast, as a counter to possible French designs. Now, in 1905, the Germans were no more sympathetic towards what they suspected to be the French intentions in that part of the world than the British had been before. Far from it. They saw no reason, and quite understandably, why France should gobble up Morocco while Germany was left out in the cold. Following the flamboyant way that the Germany of that period had of airing her grievances, the Kaiser landed at Tangier and made an inflammatory speech that set all the European chancelleries buzzing.

An immediate and dangerous crisis blew up. The press of four or five countries began to breathe fire and the General Staffs to look preoccupied. The Germans took the reasonable line of calling for an international conference, but the French for long objected. As a result, the Germans made use of some rough language, and H. A. L. Fisher declares that the German Chief of the General Staff urged that the time was ripe to force a war on France.* If so, he was overruled by higher authority, since there was no war; while the German demand for an international conference to discuss an international dispute is hardly to be cited as plain evi-

---

* H. A. L. Fisher, *History of Europe*, Vol. III, p. 1082.

dence of warlike intention. Nor was belligerent talk confined to Germany. The French Minister, Delcassé, was for war; and in England the First Sea Lord was pressing for the "Copenhagening" of the German fleet by a surprise attack without prior declaration of hostilities.

In the end, the French gave way and a conference was convened; when the Germans found to their dismay that they were in an obviously packed assembly. In fact, both Britain and Spain had secret agreements with France to let her take over the lion's share of Morocco. So had Italy, a member of the Triple Alliance. Russia was France's open ally; while the United States, though probably not fully aware of the clandestine understandings about Morocco mentioned above, had very long-standing ties of friendship with France which inclined the President and State Department to support the French point of view on any question where American interests were not involved, as was the case here. The smaller nations represented at the conference tended to follow the majority of the Great Powers and also sided with France. Germany was left very much in a minority, and suffered a bad diplomatic defeat. Only Austria and Morocco voted with her; although it is not unimportant that the latter country, which after all was the one most concerned, was in favour of the German proposals.

Nevertheless, the French were delayed in the pursuit of their ultimate objective, and it was another five years before they felt ready for the final act of military occupation of the Moroccan capital and the control of the country.* There were, of course, convenient excuses for the expedition which set forth for Fez in 1911. The Germans, however, did not believe in

* Outside the small Spanish zone.

their authenticity but regarded the expedition as a deliberate breach of the undertakings France had entered into at the Conference of 1906, as it undoubtedly was. Once more, the Germans took a spectacular way of advertising their disapproval. They sent a warship to the Moroccan port of Agadir.

This happened also to be Britain's time-honoured method of asserting her rights, but when done by the Germans it raised a storm. Again war came near, and it was on this occasion that Mr. Lloyd George made the defiant speech to Germany that was mentioned in Chapter 1. Mr. Lloyd George spoke of Britain's vital interests being challenged by the appearance of a German gunboat on the Moroccan Atlantic coast. He had evidently forgotten that, only a few years before, Britain had actually invited Germany to threaten her vital interests in that way.

Mr. Lloyd George was equally in error about the German intentions. It is now accepted that Germany had no thought of seizing a port in Morocco, either to threaten or not to threaten Britain's maritime position.* Germany was prepared to see France overrun Morocco; but if so, she would have to compensate Germany elsewhere. The latter had come late into the scramble for territory in Africa, but she saw no reason why she should not have her portion, in which sentiment the present author at least can sympathise with her. Britain, after all, had traded Morocco for Egypt in 1904. Germany was now, in 1911, ready to trade Morocco for a slice of the Congo, and the gunboat sent to Agadir was just her manner of announcing that she could not be ignored in the division of African terri-

---

* Actually, a German port on the Atlantic coast of Morocco would inevitably have fallen into British or French hands soon after an outbreak of war, a point which Mr. Lloyd George evidently overlooked. Mr. Churchill made the same mistake about Dakar in 1940.

tory. Again, it does not seem an altogether unreasonable attitude.

In the end, the Agadir crisis was solved by direct negotiation between France and Germany on the Congo-for-Morocco basis. There is no evidence that Germany wanted war over the issue, and the Russian Ambassador in Berlin reported at the time that the Kaiser was determined it should not come to war. One of the most provocative and dangerous attitudes was undoubtedly that of England, notably in the case of the Lloyd George speech and Sir Edward Grey's repeated assurances to France that Britain would back her up "to the end."

We can now turn to the other crisis point at the other end of Europe—the Balkans. The trouble-maker here was Serbia, encouraged by Russia. The Balkan peoples were of mixed origin, but the Serbs and Bulgars were Slavs, kindred to the Russians. The most numerous and perhaps the most vigorous were the Serbs, who inhabited a large area north of Greece extending north-west up the coast of the Adriatic towards Venetia. This area had once been divided between the Western and Eastern Roman Empires, the former based on Rome, and the latter on Constantinople. The Ottoman Turks had overthrown the Eastern Empire in 1453, and during the next two centuries had expanded north-west into Europe until they reached the gates of Vienna, where they were stopped. Their decline then set in, and gradually over the next two and a half centuries they were forced back, some of the territory they lost passing to Austria. But at the beginning of the twentieth century, much of the Balkans, including Thrace, Herzogovina, Bulgaria, Bosnia, Albania, and Rumania, was still nominally Turkish.

Of these, Bulgaria was practically independent, and Bosnia and Herzogovina were administered by Austria. But in the Turkish-controlled areas of Thrace and Macedonia, the misgovernment could hardly have been worse, being a scandalous tale of corruption, stagnating inefficiency, and frequent massacre. It was only a question of time before the Christian Balkan States combined to deliver their co-religionists from Turkish brutality and misrule.

The Serbs, who had gained their independence of the Sultan in 1878, were not only interested in driving the Turks out of Europe. They had their eye on Austria as well. The Austrian Empire might well become, in their view, the second "sick man of Europe" after the Ottoman Empire had expired or been given the *coup de grace*.

The Austrian (or rather the Austro-Hungarian) Empire was, as previously mentioned in Chapter 3, a hotch-potch of mixed racial groups. Austria proper was Teutonic. To the north was Bohemia, inhabited by Czechs and Slovaks of Slav stock. To the east were the Magyar Hungarians, and to the south and south-east, bordering on the Adriatic, were Slovenes and Croats, whom the Serbs claimed as fellow Slavs. The Serb ultra-nationalists in Belgrade had long-term plans to unite with these Adriatic southern Slavs in a greater Serbia.

Russia, being the Slav homeland, naturally viewed these Serbian aspirations with approval, more especially as they postulated a Serbian ally against Russia's neighbour and traditional enemy, Austria. Russia established close relations with the Serbian Government and gave it all the encouragement she could in its expansionist aims. There was also a specifically Russian advantage to be gained from the dismemberment of Austria at the hands of Serbia, backed by Russia. It might lead to the long-sought Russian control of the Bosphorus and the Dardanelles.

But both Russia and Serbia needed time before they would be ready for launching an anti-Austrian campaign. Russia had suffered severely in the war against the Japanese in 1904-05 and could not recover sufficiently to face a major war in Europe in support of Serbia for a number of years. And the Serbs first of all had to arrange for the elimination of possible intervention by the Turkish Army before it was safe to deal with Austria; that army being, from past experience, a force not to be despised.

The Austrians, through their intelligence system, were well aware of Serbia's hostile and aggressive intentions and of Russia's complicity therewith. They were faced with an unpleasant problem. Austria would get no stronger with the passage of time, but Russia would and so would Serbia. If Austria were to wait until she was attacked it would play into her enemies' hands by enabling them to strike at their own selected moment. The alternative was to force a preventive war on Serbia before Russia was fully prepared for war and deal Serbia a blow from which she would not quickly recover. But this line of action undoubtedly involved the danger of a general European conflagration, and in any case would require the concurrence of Germany, which might not be forthcoming.

There were strong advocates in Austria of a preventive war against Serbia; but they had not prevailed before the Serbs made their first move. In 1912, the Balkan League of Serbia, Bulgaria, and Greece struck at Turkey. The Turks were quickly defeated and driven back almost to Constantinople, but the peace treaty left them with a tiny strip of territory covering that city.

The Turkish Army was now out of the way. There followed a war among the Balkan victors over the division of the spoils. But from this, too, Serbia emerged victorious. Though she needed time to recuperate after her efforts, the stage was now set for her next move, this time against Austria.

5

Who Started the First World War?

On June 28th, 1914, in the year following the conclusion of the Balkan wars, the Archduke Franz Ferdinand, heir to the aged Emperor of Austria, was assassinated with his wife when on a visit to Sarajevo in Bosnia, a Slav province of Austria which Serbia coveted for her own. Bosnia had formerly been under Turkish rule but had been occupied by Austria, with the agreement of Russia, in 1877. Austria had been granted the further right, acknowledged by the powers in conference at Berlin in 1878, to annex the province whenever she wished. She exercised this right in 1908, for reasons connected with the "Young Turk" revolution of that year in Constantinople. The annexation raised a storm of indignation in Serbia, where there was a clamour for war against Austria. The Archduke Franz Ferdinand, it may be added, was known to be of a liberal and conciliatory disposition and might be expected when he came to the throne, as he obviously soon would in view of his father's advanced age, to do all he could to reconcile the Slav portions of his Empire to Austrian rule.

The assassination, which the Austrians then believed (and which is now generally agreed) to have been connived at, if not organised, by the Serbian Government, came to the Austrian Government as the culminating provocation of the Serbian challenge. The Austrian statesmen knew that the Serbs had for years been plotting the break-up of the Austrian Empire, and that in this they were being abetted by Russia. Rightly or wrongly, the Austrian authorities came to the conclusion that the assassination of the Archduke marked the decisive point in the Austro-Serbian question. Unless the Austrian Empire was passively to allow itself to be dismembered piecemeal, the time had come to make a stand against Serbian aggression. If Serbia's menacing intentions were to be frustrated she must be taught a sharp lesson.

Is Austria seriously to be blamed for adopting this attitude? Not at all. She had a better historical claim to Bosnia than had Serbia, since it had for long periods before the arrival of the Turks been either part of the Western Empire or of the Kingdom of Hungary, now joined with Austria under one Emperor. For these same historical reasons, the Bosnians were Roman Catholics where they were not Moslems, whereas the Serbs were of the Greek church.

After waiting nearly a month, the Austrians sent Serbia a very stiff note on July 23, 1914, demanding various drastic measures to end anti-Austrian agitation and hostile activity.

What would Britain have done? When faced with an analogous situation in Ireland in 1920, she proceeded to act in much the same way as Austria in 1914, by bringing the strongest coercion to bear on the Irish

Republican Army that was openly trying to free Ireland from British rule. Long-drawn-out and ruthless operations were conducted against the Irish guerrilla forces, in which terrible atrocities were perpetrated by both sides, on the British mainly by a special force of "Black and Tans" recruited from the gangster types. In the middle of the campaign, Mr. Lloyd George, the Prime Minister, declared publicly that "there would be no shaking hands with murder." Yet in the end he did shake hands with it, partly because it was proving so tough an antagonist in Ireland and partly because the Americans were twisting the lion's tail on the other side of the Atlantic. But had the Prince of Wales been assassinated by Irish gunmen while on a visit to Dublin, it cannot be doubted that the Anglo-Irish struggle would have been even bitterer and more prolonged.

The peculiar danger of the Austrian action was, of course, that it might involve all Europe in war. Russia was known to be backing Serbia, so that punitive action by Austria against the latter might bring in the Russians. Russia's entry would bring in Germany and perhaps Italy on the side of Austria, which in turn would involve France in support of Russia and possibly Britain too. Was Austria, then, to do nothing against the assassins of her Imperial heir, or nothing to check the continual and avowed sapping by the Serbs of the Imperial foundations? If so, it meant that, faced with unquestionably aggressive intentions on the part of a neighbour, she was to be denied the right to defend herself.

The question of whether Austrian action against Serbia was to result in a general war really depended on Russia's reaction. If Russia abstained from aiding Serbia, peace might be saved. It is known that

Germany had no wish for war, nor Britain. It is true that Germany did not discourage Austria, anyhow in the early stages of the crisis, from taking drastic action against the Serbs. But Germany could hardly have done otherwise. Her whole strategical policy was based on the Triple Alliance of herself, Austria, and Italy. In Italian loyalty she had no confidence, and with just cause. There remained Austria as Germany's probable sole support. If the Serbs were to continue unhampered their intrigues and plans to destroy the Austrian Empire, they might succeed in doing so; and this would leave Germany alone to confront a hostile combination of France, Russia, and probably Britain. It was to Germany's vital interest that the Austrian Empire be kept intact, and therefore that Serb conspiracies be held under control.

Englishmen of the 1914 generation will recall the then popular view of Germany as the European military colossus, terrorising other nations by the menace of her huge army. A dispassionate examination of the strategical facts of the case may, however, suggest that the picture looked quite different through German eyes. The pre-war estimates of war strengths of the various armies gave the Franco-Russian combination *an excess* over the German-Austrian combination that varied from 700,000 to 1,200,000 men; and there is evidence that, in spite of all their seeming arrogance and swashbuckling confidence, the Germans were governed by a genuine fear of Russia's millions of soldiers. This may seem hard to credit in the after-light of the pitiful Russian collapse in the war. But it has to be remembered that dangers seem always particularly formidable in prospect. The British, with a decisive lead in naval power, felt anxious enough over the challenge of the *inferior* German fleet; so anxious

that the challenge drove them into the arms of France
and Russia, the two chief traditional enemies of the
British past. No Briton therefore has the right to question that Germany could have felt grave concern at
the menace of the *superior* Russian Army.* Nor will
the reader need to be convinced of the acute concern
which has dominated the whole of the Western world,
including the United States on the other side of the
Atlantic, during the last five to eight years, over the
reported huge size of the present-day Russian military machine.

If, however, Germany had good grounds for regarding the assassination of the Archduke Franz Ferdinand
as pregnant with menace not only to Austria but to
herself, there is reason to suppose that to Russia it
came as a welcome opportunity. To her it must have
appeared as the spark which might be fanned into
the flame of that general European war which there
is now strong cause to think both she and France had
previously determined to provoke, Russia to obtain
Constantinople and the Straits and France to regain
Alsace and Lorraine. Or not so much Russia and
France as Sazanov and Poincaré and their respective pro-war supporters; for as Sir Patrick Hastings
has said, "war is the creation of individuals not of
nations."†

The respective interests of Austria, Germany, and
Russia in regard to the assassination crisis should now
be fairly plain. Austria believed that Serbian intrigues
and ambitions constituted a deadly menace to the
continued existence of her Empire, as they undoubtedly did, and she was aware that she must either

---

* In 1914, the peace strengths of both the Russian and French armies were
greater than that of the German.

† Sir Patrick Hastings—*Autobiography*, p. 52.

curb the capacity of Serbia for further anti-Austrian mischief or see the Empire perish, and that probably soon. And if action had to be taken some time, the assassination of the Austrian heir to the throne by admittedly Serbian terrorists offered as favourable an issue on which to base that action as could be expected. The Austrians were therefore determined to force matters to a head. Resolute action at once might succeed. But if not, if it precipitated a European war, if indeed this war were to be disastrous for Austria —well, if the Austro-Hungarian Empire had to go down anyway, it might as well go down fighting. This line of argument may or may not have justified the action that the Austrian authorities took in 1914; but at least it is an understandable one.

As to Germany, it was to her interest to localise the Austro-Serbian dispute, so that the Serbs might be suitably dealt with by the Austrians without anyone else being involved.* Russia, on the other hand, was interested in the support of Serbia and was also resolved to use the Sarajevo assassination to bring on a general war, as her actions during the crisis clearly indicate.

It has been the fashion among British historians to describe the Serbian reply to the Austrian note as extraordinarily conciliatory, all but two of the Austrian demands being conceded. The present author does not take that view. The two rejected demands were the key ones that alone could have made the rest effective. All the remainder, even if nominally complied with, could easily have been evaded in practice and reduced to nullity by the Serbs. The Serbian

---

* One of the proposed Austrian means of doing so, which might or might not have been carried out in practice, was to distribute portions of Serb territory among the Bulgars, Greeks and Rumanians.

reply, which was unquestionably drawn up with the advice of France and probably Russia, could therefore be regarded as a very skilful one designed, without making any genuine concession, to put the onus of war guilt on to the Austrians.* But the Austrians wanted only the barest excuse for breaking off relations.

The Serbian reply was handed in at 6 P.M. on July 25, 1914. Before this time, however, the Russians had decided on undertaking the preliminary stages of mobilisation, which were commenced the next day. On July 28, at 11 A.M., Austria declared war on Serbia. Immediately, the Russians ordered a further stage of mobilisation. At this time, Germany had done nothing about mobilising. Nor did she on this day. On the contrary, the Kaiser sent word to the General Staff that a war was unlikely. Moreover, a telegram was sent to the German Ambassador in Vienna to urge moderation on the Austrian Government.

On July 29, the German General Staff, knowing that partial Russian mobilisation had commenced, sent a memorandum to the Kaiser pointing out the danger of German inaction in the face of Russian military preparation. But no mobilisation was ordered for Germany on that day or even the next, a forbearance that showed, in the opinion of Lowes Dickenson,† that at that stage "Germany was sincere in her effort to avoid war. What defeated that effort was the course of events in Russia."

For on the evening of 29 July, total mobilisation of the Russian Army was decided on, though it was countermanded at the last moment by the order of the Tsar, on his own initiative, after receiving a telegram from the Kaiser urging restraint. By this time,

---

* The nature of the Austrian demands on Serbia is given in Appendix 2.

† G. Lowes Dickenson, *International Anarchy, 1904-1914*, p. 447.

Russia's military measures were known in Paris and London, and Sir Edward Grey had warned the German Ambassador that in the event of a general war, Britain could be expected to enter the fight on the side of France and Russia against Germany and Austria.* Strong pressure was now being put on Austria by Germany to accept mediation and to be as conciliatory as possible.

Early on July 30, the Russian Foreign Minister, in league with the Russian General Staff, began to press the Tsar to rescind his veto on total mobilisation. The Emperor held out till 4 P.M., and then gave way. The telegrams went out. The General charged with this duty then by prearrangement "disappeared," to lessen or defeat any chance of a further counter-order.

During this time, urgent appeals were being sent in two opposite directions. Sir Edward Grey, from London, was begging Germany to use all possible moderating influence on Austria; and there is plenty of evidence that this was being done. At the same time, Sir Edward was being urged repeatedly by the Germans to take similar action with Russia, and particularly over her mobilisation. The evidence that he did so is not, unfortunately, as ample as an Englishman would like.

On July 31, the Germans, having refrained for two whole days from taking precautions against the Russian mobilisation, could afford to wait no longer. The news of total Russian mobilisation, ordered at 6 P.M. on July 30, did not reach Berlin till 11.30 A.M. the next day. By 1.45 P.M., a similar order had gone out for Germany.

---

* *The International Anarchy*, p. 453. Grey was shortly after to tell the House of Commons that Britain was uncommitted and free to enter the war, or not, as she chose.

Two hours later, Germany sent an ultimatum to Russia to cancel her mobilisation. This ultimatum may seem to put the responsibility for the actual commencement of the general war on Germany's shoulders. But, in fairness, there is this to be said for her. The total mobilisation of two countries in the state of near hostility to each other that Russia and Germany were at this time meant, as all the then General Staffs were agreed, inevitable war between them. If war were to come, it was naturally of vital importance for each country concerned to gain every possible advantage it could for the success of its own arms. One of the cardinal advantages Germany had over Russia was a more efficient and quicker mobilisation system, and to make full use of that advantage Germany needed to strike at her enemy the instant her mobilisation was complete. This was particularly so in regard to a more numerous enemy like Russia who, if given time to complete her mobilisation before being attacked, would be able to bring her greater numbers to bear with the most effect. Actually, the German plan for a Franco-Russian war was to demolish the French first, and turn on the Russians second. But the time factor remained just as urgently important. Hence, the necessity for the German ultimatum. The Russians, if left to themselves, would probably delay the declaration of war until all their far-flung manpower had assembled on the German frontier, and the German advantage of quicker mobilisation had thus been eliminated. It was vitally important for the Germans to forestall them.

It is, I think, fairly clear that the progress towards a general European flare-up was determined by Russia. Had she not mobilised, it can be taken as fairly certain that Germany would not have done so either; and as long as neither Russia nor she had taken this final and fatal step, there was always a chance of the Austro-Serbian war being localised. The Russian initiative in mobilisation was not forced upon her by compelling necessity. Her security was in no wise threatened by the Austro-Serbian conflict. The Austrians had even assured the Russian Government that any punitive measures they might adopt against Serbia did not include the acquisition of Serbian territory for themselves; and though the Russians could legitimately have disbelieved them, we know that the Austrian Ministers were opposed to the inclusion of any more of those turbulent Serbs in the Empire. In any case, the Austro-Serb situation could obviously develop a long way before Russia's own safety began to be in jeopardy. But Russia would not wait; and there is no doubt that her precipitate mobilisation was determined by ambition and not by fear. And also by the confident assurance of French support.*

At this point, we come back to the question of France and the "butcher-bird." This was the second occasion on which, according to the legend, innocent France was wantonly attacked by a predatory Germany. At the same time as they sent their ultimatum to Russia, the Germans sent one also to France, well aware of the Franco-Russian alliance and knowing that hostilities against Russia would involve also hostilities against France. Since this was an inevitable outcome of the situation that had arisen, one might think that the French, if they had been anxious to avoid war, would have put pressure on their Russian

* Gooch and Temperley—"*British Documents on the Origin of the War,*" No. 125.

allies not to force the issue? But the French not only had taken no mollifying action of this kind at St. Petersburg; they actually, though secretly, encouraged the Russians on to extreme measures.

Why did the French thus work for war? For two reasons. When M. Poincaré became President in 1912, he made it clear to the Russians that they could count on French military support *in all circumstances,** whether Russia were being attacked or whether she herself were doing the attacking. And this comprehensive assurance of the President's was undoubtedly due to his determination to bring on a general war as the only way of recovering Alsace and Lorraine, and to the prevailing belief on the part of the French General Staff that France and Russia would beat Germany and Austria.† It was a repetition of 1870. The French Army was once more ready to the last gaiter button: the French Generals supremely confident of victory.

Alas, they had miscalculated for the second time: and for the second time the fault for this cannot be laid at the Germans' door. The French strategy was based on the theory of "the unconditional offensive," the magic qualities of which would quickly carry the French Army to Berlin. But the true qualities of the theory proved to be more suicidal than magical and led mainly to fearful slaughter among the French troops. In a matter of days, the French war plan was in ruins and the French Army, instead of advancing into Germany, was in wholesale retreat towards Paris. The French had also overestimated the military value of their Russian allies, which was revealed as far below expectations.

* Lowes Dickenson, *"The International Anarchy,"* pp. 329-334.

† See, inter alia, Benckendorff to Sazanov, 25-2-1913.

If anyone was to blame for the invasion of France by the Germans in 1914, it was the French themselves. Had their President thrown the weight of his influence into dissuading the Russians from hurrying into warlike preparations, instead of egging them on, it is quite likely there would have been no Armageddon. But Poincaré and the war party were hankering after revenge for the débâcle of 1870, were resolutely set on regaining the lost provinces of Alsace and Lorraine, and had once again mesmerised themselves into the belief that they were the heirs of the great Napoleon's victorious Grande Armée. They were, in fact, anxious for war.

As for the Germans having started the 1914 war, there could be no greater myth, in the author's opinion, based on the available evidence. If any nation could, in his view, be said to have "started" the war in the sense of taking the first steps which led to hostilities, it was Serbia for the Austro-Serbian war, and Russia for the larger conflict. Had the Serbs eschewed their "Greater Serbia" ambitions, there seems to be no reason why they and the Austrians should ever have come into collision. As I see it, the Serbs were the primary aggressors and the original causers of the First World War. But they were closely seconded by the Russians, who were the initial agents in converting a local conflict into a global disaster. Whether the Serbs were culpable in planning and working for a "Greater Serbia" object, and the Russians in encouraging them, is another matter altogether, which I shall not argue. The point here is whether the Germans "started" the 1914 war, as has often been alleged against them, and I think the truth is otherwise.

The original participants in that war can be divided into two classes: those who looked for positive gain from a European war and those who desired only to keep what they had. In the first class were the Serbs, the Russians, and the French, and two of the three eventually received the booty they coveted. In the second class were the Austrians and the Germans, who for that reason had more to lose and therefore—especially in Germany's case—less incentive to want a general war than the others. In that ill-starred summer of 1914, I should say that of all the European Great Powers those who wanted war the least were the Germans and the British.

So much venom has been hurled against Prussian militarism in the last forty to fifty years that it comes as something of a shock to discover that at the height of the 1914 crisis the German General Staff addressed a memorandum to its Government on July 29, which contained sentiments of a most admirably balanced, farseeing, and statesmanlike character. "Russia has announced," the German Generals said, "that she will mobilise against Austria if Austria invades Serbia. Austria will therefore have to mobilise against Russia. The collision between the two States will then have become inevitable. But that, for Germany, is the *casus foederis*. She therefore must mobilise, too. Russia will then mobilise the rest of her forces. She will say: 'I am being attacked by Germany.' Thus, the Franco-Russian Alliance, so often held up to praise as a purely defensive compact, created only to meet the aggressive plans of Germany, will become active and the mutual butchery of the civilised nations of Europe will begin. . . . After this fashion things must and will develop, unless, one might say, a miracle happens to prevent at the last moment a war which will annihilate for decades the civilisation of almost all Europe." *

Is it possible, after reading the above extract, to continue to regard the German General Staff as nothing more than jack-booted, goose-stepping, sabre-rattlers; or as a criminal organisation such as the prosecution at Nuremberg tried to stamp them? Not for me, anyway. I know of no other General Staff at this time that showed any such reluctance as is instinct in the German memorandum. Sir Henry Wilson's Diaries portray him either as licking his lips at the prospect of a war or tearing his hair at the possibility that Britain might not enter it.

The forecast in the German General Staff memorandum was all too accurate. There was, indeed, only one error. The Russians did not wait for German mobilisation to order total mobilisation for themselves. They did it first—by 20 hours.

Finally, let me give the verdicts on the question of war responsibility of three historians, an Englishman, an American, and a Frenchman. The Englishman, G. Lowes Dickenson, sums the question up as follows:

". . . we must enquire which has the greater justification—a State (Austria) which is defending itself against disruption, or one (Serbia) which is desirous to extend its power by the disruption of its neighbour. That really was the question between Austria and Russia. I should answer myself . . . that the justification lies with Austria and the aggression with Russia.

We next come to Germany. Against her has been directed most of the moral indignation of the victorious Powers. That this is not justified by the facts should be clear, after our analysis. . . . The Powers of the Entente

* Quoted by Lowes Dickenson in his *International Anarchy*, pp. 445 & 446.

say that the offence was Germany's backing of Austria.
Germans say that the offence was Russia's backing of Serbia.
. . . To my mind, the German position is the more
reasonable."*

Secondly, here is the opinion of the distinguished
American historian, Dr. H. E. Barnes. Summarising
the relative responsibility for the war in his detailed
study of the evidence, Dr. Barnes says:

"In estimating the order of guilt of the various countries
we may safely say that the only direct and immediate
responsibility for the world war falls upon Serbia, France
and Russia, with the guilt about equally distributed. Next
in order—far below France and Russia—would come Austria, though she never desired a general European war.
Finally, we should place England and Germany, in the
order named, both being opposed to war in the 1914 crisis.
Probably the German public was somewhat more favourable to military activities than the English people, but, as
we have amply explained above, the Kaiser made more
strenuous efforts to preserve the peace of Europe than did
Sir Edward Grey." †

Lastly, the Frenchman, M. Morhardt, has this to
say about President Poincaré's visit to Russia in July,
1914, at the height of the Sarajevo crisis:

"The fact alone of undertaking such a trip at such a time
meant a plan for war. . . . If M. Raymond Poincaré
wanted peace, a letter to St. Petersburg would have sufficed. If Russia had been warned that France was resolved
not to espouse, before the world, the cause of the assassins
at Sarajevo, the whole matter would have been solved.

---

* *The International Anarchy*, pp. 478, 479.

† Harry Elmer Barnes, *The Genesis of the World War*, Knopf, pp. 661,
662.

Peace would have been maintained. Never if he [M. Poincaré] had not gone to preach savagely the war crusade in St. Petersburg, as M. Maurice Paléologue has told us, would the cowardly Nicholas II have dared to take the aggressive initiative."*

* M. Morhardt, *Les Preuves,* pp. 299-301.

6

Germany and Poland
(1939)

The war of 1914-18 demonstrated for the second time
in succession that the French were capable of gross
strategical miscalculations. They had believed in a
quick war of conquest in 1870 and in 1914. And they
were disastrously wrong on both occasions. In 1870 they
were decisively beaten in a few months. In 1914 the
Russian steam-roller, on which they pinned so much
faith that they urged it into premature motion against
Germany, turned out to be a mass of leaky joints, worn
bearings and faulty adjustments. By 1917 it was on
the scrap-heap, and in the same year the French Army
mutinied. France would have been beaten again had
it not been for the presence on French soil of more
than two million British soldiers, who kept the Germans occupied while the French recovered their discipline. The biggest British Army fighting on the
Continent in Wellington's time had not exceeded
70,000 men. Allowing for the difference in size of population, the 1914 equivalent was 280,000. In the six
years of the Peninsular War, 40,000 British soldiers lost

their lives. In the four years of the First World War, there were 750,000 deaths. Mr. Haldane's "scientific" method of waging war by linking up with the French had increased the British military effort ten times and the death-roll twenty times. It can be argued that without this vast effort and huge loss of life the Germans would have won the war. But had not the French been given so many unofficial assurances that the British Army would be at their side in a war against Germany, it is possible that that war would not have occurred. Moreover, it has already been argued that the defeat of France by no means involved the defeat of England; as, indeed, the Second World War demonstrated.

By 1918 the French were taking the line that they had been wickedly attacked by the Germans, and loudly demanded guarantees for their future security against such brigandage. Their British and American colleagues at the peace negotiations uncritically accepted these demands and agreed that Germany must be disarmed, militarily and economically; and so she was. Furthermore, the Austrian Empire was broken up, and the new states of Poland and Czechoslovakia were created, bordering Germany on the east and south.* With these two succession States France proceeded to conclude alliances. France thus adopted the dangerous policy of peace by repression, of keeping her chief rival permanently weak and under surveillance. The French had got back the partly German provinces of Alsace and Lorraine and took as well the wholly German coal area of the Saar.

This policy had lasted for fifteen years when the law

---

* The separate state of Hungary and a greatly enlarged Serbia, with the title of Jugoslavia, were also created out of the ruins of the Austrian Empire.

of action and reaction asserted itself. The Germans, who had proved themselves in the war by far the best fighting nation of Europe, grew tired of the state of subjection to which they had been reduced and put the Nazis into power. This was the inevitable outcome of the French policy of repression.

Germany under the Nazis proceeded to rearm; and, for participating in this re-armament, individual Germans were charged at the Nuremberg trials with criminal breaches of the Treaty of Versailles. Were these charges justified? I do not think so. The disarmament of Germany, decreed in 1919, was declared at the time not to be solely for the purpose of drawing Germany's military teeth. It was said to be "the first step towards the reduction and limitation of armaments (of all nations) which (the Allied and Associated Powers) seek to bring about as one of the most fruitful preventives of war. . . ." How many tongues were in the Allied and Associated cheeks at this declaration, I do not know. It soon became clear, however, that if any of the victorious powers were anxious to disarm, the French were not among them. They maintained a large conscript army, conscription being forbidden to the Germans.

By 1927, Mr. Lloyd George, the chief British representative at the Peace Conference, was becoming uncomfortable. He referred in Parliament to the "nations which had pledged themselves to disarmament, following the German example," but which "had taken no steps to disarm." And he was by no means alone in his misgivings.

Five years later, in 1932, came the much publicised Disarmament Conference at Geneva. It was a complete failure. Nevertheless, the late victorious Powers expected Germany to go on faithfully observing the German disarmament clauses of the Treaty of Versailles. It was by now obvious to the world, and must have been particularly obvious to the Germans, that the "general disarmament" pledge of the Versailles Treaty was fraudulent. No nation was going to disarm down to Germany's level. Disarmament was evidently to apply to her alone, and apparently in perpetuity.

The Germans had been tricked. The victorious nations did not mean to disarm. It is true that disarmament could have been imposed on Germany by *force majeure* alone. But the victorious nations had refrained from doing this. They had voluntarily stated that they, too, would disarm. But, by 1933, when Hitler gained power, they had made it plain that they meant to dishonour their pledge.

No great nation, even if it has been an unquestionable aggressor, can be expected to accept a state of bondage indefinitely. If it does not consider itself an aggressor, though its enemies may say it is, it will be even less inclined to submit to such a role. Hitler reached power in Germany largely on the promise to rescue his country from that bondage and restore it to sovereign freedom. This he achieved, by a combination of shrewd political boldness, bluff, and prevarication. For his repeated public falsehoods, especially in his declarations about his claims on foreign countries, he was bitterly assailed as a blatant liar. It could, however, have been advanced in his defence that Germany's former foes had lied as seriously to her about their intention to disarm; and not only about this. In January, 1918, President Wilson of the United States had enunciated Fourteen Points in a speech to the Congress as the basis of a lasting peace to follow the war then in progress. In the following September, the Germans made an offer of peace in accordance with those Fourteen Points. This was accepted by the President on behalf of his allies, it being specifically agreed that Germany was treating for peace on the lines of the Fourteen Points in question. But no sooner had the Germans complied with the disarmament clauses of the Armistice than the victors proceeded to scrap the condition that the Fourteen Points were to be the guide for the peace treaty. It is pleasant to record that shocked protests were made in Britain at this breach of faith. Thus, Lord Buckmaster declared that:

"to induce any nation, however evil and abominable they might be, to lay down their arms on one set of terms and then, when they were defenceless, to impose another set, is an act of dishonour which can never be effaced."

The British conscience and sense of honour was still fairly active at that date (1922).

If, then, deliberate chicanery was employed towards Germany in relation to her terms of surrender, and later in order to keep her weak as long as possible, it was surely no worse for Hitler to use deceit to make Germany strong as quickly as possible. One set of lies can be held to justify another set in international politics. But the bulk of the British critics who were rabid about Hitler's use of the lie as a strategical weapon had probably never heard of the Fourteen Points trickery or of the "general disarmament" clause of the Treaty of Versailles. Their indignation was thus comprehensible, even if misplaced.

By the end of 1938 Hitler, mainly by his own personal initiative and even against the opposition of the General Staff, had resurrected a conscript German Army and Air Force, recovered the Rhineland, absorbed Austria, and annexed Czechoslovakia. He had almost nullified the anti-German features of the Versailles Treaty, to the Germans' natural delight.

There remained, apart from the colonies, the matters of Alsace-Lorraine and the Polish Corridor. Hitler said he had no quarrel with Poland; but such a statement had so often been the prelude to an attack on the country named that no one knew whether to believe him or not.

The British Government was by this time being pressed very hard to do something to "stop Hitler"; and on March 21st, 1939, it very unwisely gave a guarantee to Poland. On September 1, Hitler sent his army against Poland and conquered her in under three weeks. As a result, the British, in obedience to their guarantee, declared war on Germany on September 3, followed later in the day and with obvious reluctance by the French. It was in consequence of Hitler's attack on Poland in the face of the British guarantee and therefore with the certainty of the extension of the war to the major Powers, that he has been accused of starting the Second World War. This, however, is too facile a judgment.

First of all, was there anything essentially wicked in Hitler's desire to retake the Polish Corridor? If there was, the wickedness was no greater than France's relentless ambition from 1870 to 1918 to recover Alsace and Lorraine. Alsace and Lorraine were almost as much German as French, although before 1870 they had been part of France for 220 and 100 years respectively. But, in the same way, the Polish Corridor had been German territory for the best part of a century and a half; it contained many Germans as well as Poles, and its reversion to the recreated Poland in 1919 separated East Prussia from the rest of Germany and involved the isolation and semi-ruin of the important and wholly German city of Danzig. Germany obviously had as good a claim to the Corridor as France had to Alsace and Lorraine. And since the victors at Versailles, who included both the British and the French, had recognised this right of prior possession in France's favour in regard to the two provinces, their charge of criminal aggression against Germany—and certain German individuals—for applying the same type of claim to the Polish Corridor was plainly hypocritical.

But what of the associated question of bringing on a major war? It is very easy to jump to the conclusion that a country which attacks a guaranteed territory must be guilty of provoking the larger conflict that ensues. But more careful thought suggests two reasons why such an assumption may be dangerously superficial. For one thing, it is too easy a way of putting a potential adversary in the wrong. All that a great Power has to do when it believes its special territorial interests are about to be challenged by another is to scatter guarantees over those territories in order to turn its challengers automatically into world criminals. This would have worked out very awkwardly for Britain in the days when she was the challenging power; as, for example, against Spain in the sixteenth century, Holland in the seventeenth, and Spain and France in the eighteenth.

The second reason is that a guarantee, while forming no certain barrier—as Hitler showed—to the outbreak of hostilities, may even provoke it. A guarantee is itself a challenge. It publicly dares a rival to ignore the guarantee and take the consequences; after which it is hardly possible for that rival to endeavour to seek a peaceful solution of its dispute with the guaranteed country without appearing to be submitting to blackmail. A guarantee may therefore act as an incitement to that very major conflict which it is presumably meant to prevent. It is most significant, as is made clear in F. H. Hinsley's meticulous examination of the evidence in his book *Hitler's Strategy,** that the German Dictator's determination to force the issue against Poland to the point of war dates from the very day when the British guarantee was announced.

What should we think if the Russians were to guarantee Egypt the possession of the Canal Zone, whether or not Russia were in a position to help her get it, as Britain was not in a position to help Poland keep the Corridor? Should we meekly pack up our traps and leave? Or, if we stayed, should we willingly accept the stigma of being aggressors and the "starters" of the Third World War? I think not.

As for the third German invasion of France, which took place in 1940, it was the French who had declared war against the Germans in 1939. The French Army made no attempt to aid the Poles by action against the Germans in the West. Instead, it sat tight behind its own frontier. Since 1914, there had been a complete reversal of French military ideas. From the disastrous unconditional offensive at the opening of the First World War, the French General Staff had swung hard over to the unconditional defensive. The French Army was to remain in its fortified Maginot Line and await attack. This equally rigid, though opposite, extreme of strategy fared no better than its predecessor. For the third time the French were driven back; this time, as in 1870, to final catastrophe.

We have now gained a clearer picture of the three "brutal and unprovoked" invasions of France by Germany about which the Vansittarts of this country and

* Cambridge University Press, p. 11.

the French themselves have said so many bitter things. We have the significant fact that in two out of the three cases, it was France that declared war on Germany; while, in the third, France was surreptitiously urging on her Russian ally to bring on a war with Germany in which France knew she would be involved. There is, indeed, quite a lot of evidence for holding that it was France and not Germany who, to use Lord Vansittart's phrase about the latter, "carefully contrived" the war of 1914. Moreover, in two out of the three cases, the French thought they would be in Berlin in about two months. It was their own military miscalculations and shortcomings and not German turpitude that caused the invasions to be towards Paris instead.

The French "hard-luck" stories about their ill-treatment by Germany are not true, but these stories have been swallowed whole by a gullible public which is ignorant of the historical facts of the case. And the same "hard-luck" stories are even now in use by the French to sabotage the creation of a Western German Army.

The world has heard much since 1919 of the German invasions of France. But next to nothing has been said of the French invasions of Germany. Yet for two hundred years, it was Germany that provided the battlegrounds of Europe. It was backwards and forwards over Germany and Austria that the French armies marched and fought in the wars of the eighteenth century, while the soil of France remained unravaged. And it was again on German and Austrian territory that Napoleon won his celebrated victories in the early nineteenth century.

The French do not forget about these earlier episodes in which the military glory was France's, because their statues and street-names in Paris and elsewhere abound in Wagrams, Austerlitzs, Jenas, and Friedlands. But they wish the rest of the world to forget about them and to remember only that a unified Germany is nowadays a terrible threat to France, in consequence of which it is France's persistent endeavour to get Germany broken up and weakened.

But what was the primary cause of German unification? No other than the frequent aggressions of unified France. It was the subjugation of Germany by Napoleon in 1806 that was the admitted origin of the Pan-German feeling. Against the French danger, Germans all over Europe began to draw together and acquire a wider sense of Germanic brotherhood. Whereas in 1793 there were over 300 separate and independent states in what is now Germany, these had been reduced by amalgamation to 30 by 1815. The process, once started, went on. We have noted in an earlier chapter how, after 1815, the German States formed a common consultative body in the German Confederation. The mental soil was being prepared for Bismarck's enclosures. The French, of all people, are the least entitled to complain of a German menace, for it is of their own making.

Yet, by causing enough fuss, they succeeded in getting just such a complaint taken up after 1919 as a sort of sacred object of international politics; and right up to the present day, western politicians and commentators speak as if France had a natural right to protection against Germany, the protection to be provided by the rest of the world. Thus, whenever France makes herself particularly difficult over the re-creation of a German Army or the question of German restoration as a sovereign State, there never fail to be highly placed British apologists for French intransigence who declare that "in view of all France has suffered from Germany . . . etc., etc"; for which reason, it seems, British and other youth must be ready to be sacrificed again to keep the French from being upset.

It is, of course, complete nonsense. France has no "right" to any security. No country has. We all live in a dangerous world, and if any nation wishes for security it must arrange that security for itself as best it can; by itself, or in suitable combination if it cannot be achieved alone. But the onus for all of us is on ourselves, little though the babu class which staffs the growing international bodies cares to admit the fact. After all, if the rest of the world is under an obligation to protect France against Germany, it is under an equal obligation to protect Germany against France, so that the logical outcome of gratuitous international protection is international civil war.

France has only one formula for her own protection. It is to put the clock back to the eighteenth century and keep Germany weak by keeping her divided, disarmed, and disunited. It is a formula which shows how stupid an intelligent nation can be. For the natural sequel to an attempt to keep a country like Germany permanently down is a vigorous and inevitable effort on her part to throw off the shackles of foreign control; and the greater the repression, the more violent will be the eventual upheaval in search of national freedom and self-respect.

As for the charge that Germany alone "started" both the world wars, this is quite untrue as regards the first war, and is at least questionable in regard to the second.

7

What Was
Mr. Churchill's War
Object?

If the evidence I have set out in the last six chapters is reasonably accurate, it follows that the many thousands of British men and women, including a number of my own friends and acquaintances, who still believe that Germany alone was responsible for the two world wars, which she started deliberately, wickedly, and without provocation or excuse, are gravely mistaken. It is not their fault. To reach anything like a balanced judgment on this subject requires much more historical reading than the ordinary person has time to devote to such a purpose.

We were, moreover, told repeatedly by our leaders during the war years that the Germans had done all this. Mr. Churchill, whose influence in shaping national opinion about the enemy was enormous, kept on saying that they had started both wars, in just those words. According to him, Germany was the one and only aggressor; the world pest. Mr. Churchill seemed to think that if Germany could be utterly crushed, the rest of the world could resume its peaceful ways; and that if she were kept crushed this blessed state of affairs could continue indefinitely. As he said in Parliament on 21 September, 1943:

"The twin roots of all our evils, Nazi tyranny and Prussian militarism, must be extirpated. Until this is achieved, there are no sacrifices we will not make and no lengths in violence to which we will not go."

Mr. Churchill could not, I think, have contemplated illimitability of sacrifice for his country and extremity of violence against the German enemy unless he was convinced that the extirpation of the Nazi State and the German Army would solve the problem of European security and usher in a prolonged period of peace.

In this matter of crushing Germany completely, President Roosevelt was not one whit behind Mr. Churchill. Indeed, it was the President himself who was the producer of the "unconditional surrender" plan, to which Mr. Churchill gave his support. The two leaders, American and British, achieved their joint aim. The war was continued until Germany did surrender unconditionally.

But the complete and absolute victory of the Anglo-American Allies, the necessary prelude to the intended extirpations, had hardly taken place when it crumbled into dust in their hands. The smashing of the German Reich and war machine did not remove "all our evils," as Mr. Churchill had predicted. No sooner was the German military menace out of the way than the ugly scowling form of a new danger was to be seen standing malevolently in its place. Hostile, militant Russian Communism had moved quickly into

the spot where Germany had been. Nor was it the
only disturber of the Churchillian conception of a
peace-loving world kept in a state of turbulence by
the Germans. Very soon, militant Communism forced
its way to power in China also.

Mr. Churchill's theory that "the twin roots of all our
evils" were Nazi tyranny and Prussian militarism was
thus brutally disproved almost as soon as these latter
were overthrown. Other tyrannies and other milita-
risms had come into view behind and beyond them.
Other tyrannies just as bad, if not worse; other mili-
tarisms just as voracious, if not more so. Germany,
after all, had been engaged only in recovering what
had previously been German and Austrian territories
when she was attacked by Britain and France. But
after Germany's collapse and occupation, Russia proceeded to extend her sway by a mixture of force and
subversion to include countries to which she had no
shadow of a claim: to Western Poland, to Rumania,
Bulgaria, Hungary, and Czechoslovakia. German aggression (if aggression it was) was succeeded and surpassed by Russian aggression.

The declared aim of President Roosevelt and Mr.
Churchill to end aggression by destroying the German
capacity for it was, in fact, one of the greatest failures
in history. Never before, perhaps, have so many aggressions been crowded into so short a time as have taken
place in the few years since Germany's defeat: the
Russian aggressions in Europe, the aggression by some
person or persons unknown which drove the Dutch
out of Indonesia, the Indian aggression against Hy-
derabad, the Chinese aggression against Tibet, the
North Korean aggression against South Korea, the
French aggression against Germany over the Saar, the
Chinese aggression against the United Nations in Ko-

rea, and probably several others I have overlooked.* A pretty good score for any similar period of years, and especially those immediately following the hanging of the German "butcher-bird's" corpse on the wire.

Under these repeated hammer blows of refuting circumstance, the Roosevelt-Churchill doctrine of the all-sufficing efficacy of German disarmament could not last long. In 1950, it was formally abandoned and Western Germany was asked to re-arm. By then, however, the Nuremberg War Crimes Trials, the brutal treatment of the German officer class generally, and the ruthless dismantling of German factories had induced in the Western Germans a widespread reluctance to be again drawn into warlike courses. The gracious permission to re-arm thereupon changed into a mixture of entreaties and threats which, were it not for the European devastation that had accompanied the pursuit of the opposite policy, would have been extremely comical. By 1951, Mr. Churchill's wartime views on the "roots of all our evils," to extirpate which he had demanded unlimited sacrifice and had thrown the whole resources of his country, had been completely discredited. The British electorate proceeded to celebrate this historic refutation by calling him back to office. In 1945, when the fruits of his victory were as yet unsampled and the British public had no evidence for doubting that the benefits would be as ad-

---

* I use the word 'aggression' in the loose and slipshod manner of everyday parlance. It is, however, an astonishing fact that there is no authoritative way of recognising aggression. The former League of Nations tried for twenty years to define aggression, but without success. The attempt was taken up by the United Nations, and with the same negative result. Indeed, after several years of vain endeavour and while the Korean war was actually in progress, arguments began to be heard in the United Nations' conference halls that it was unwise to define aggression at all. And, curiously enough, the chief protagonists of this view were the Americans and the British, who were also the main supporters of the war in Korea "to show that aggression did not pay."

vertised, it had thrown him out. *Vox populi vox dei.*

Something had clearly been wrong with the wartime object which Mr. Churchill had been pursuing, and it is very desirable to discover the nature of the defect. But before that question can be answered, it is necessary to know with some precision what Mr. Churchill's wartime object was. We have taken note of two possible claimants to the title, but it will be as well to look at any others. There was, for instance, the declaration of aims by him and the American President, embodied in the document known as the Atlantic Charter and issued to the world in August 1941. In this Charter, the two leaders said that they desired to see no territorial changes that did not accord with the freely expressed wishes of the peoples concerned. This was Article 2 of the Charter. But in due course, large areas of Poland were given to Russia and similar areas of Germany were given to Poland without the Polish and German inhabitants of those areas having their wishes even consulted.

Article 3 said that the two leaders respected the right of *all peoples* to choose the form of Government under which they would live. Unless the words "all peoples" did not mean all peoples, this Article clearly applied as much to the Germans as to anyone else. But two years later, Mr. Churchill was declaring that one of the "roots of all our evils" was Nazi tyranny, which must be extirpated. The choice of the Germans to live under a National Socialist government was therefore barred; so that Mr. Churchill's declaration of September 1943 contradicted Article 3 of his declaration of August 1941. Indeed, Article 6 of the Charter had the same effect.

Article 4 of the Charter said that endeavour would be made to further the "enjoyment by all States, great or small, *victor or vanquished,* of access, *on equal terms,* to the trade and to the raw materials of the world, which are needed for their economic prosperity. Unless the word "vanquished" does not mean vanquished and the words "on equal terms" do not mean on equal terms, no attempt has been made to honour this purely voluntary undertaking to Germany up to the time of writing.

Article 6 of the Charter began with the words, "after the final destruction of Nazi tyranny," which were incompatible with the freedom promised in Article 3 to *all peoples.* Article 6 went on to say that the two leaders hoped for a peace which will afford *all nations* the means of dwelling in safety within their own boundaries. Yet both leaders later agreed to conditions which involved the expulsion of large numbers of Germans from lands where they had lived from antiquity, the actual number of those expelled amounting in the event, it is said, to the enormous total of fifteen millions.

I have not quoted all the Articles of the Charter. There were several others in the same vein. But these are the most relevant ones. They breathe, I think, a spirit of moderation and fair-dealing, of equal treatment to winners and losers alike; the only directly discordant note being the conflict between Articles 3 and 6 already referred to. Yet, as my passing comments on the various articles indicate, there was a chasm between the Anglo-American promise of 1941 and the victors' performance from 1945 onwards.

The explanation is that the Atlantic Charter did not last the length of the war. In February 1944, it was publicly repudiated by Mr. Churchill, who declared that there was no question of it "applying to Germany as a matter of right and banning territorial transferences or adjustments in any countries." Certainly it did not apply to Germany as a matter of right. But the Charter did apply to her for no less potent a reason. This was that the good name of the British people was involved in its application to her. They had raised no word of protest when Mr. Churchill (with the American President) had proclaimed that the principles of the Charter were to apply to *all nations, all peoples, all States, great or small, victor or vanquished.*" By thus acquiescing, the British nation had accepted obligations of honour to apply the Charter provisions to Germany as much as to anyone else. Mr. Churchill, therefore, by announcing in 1944 that the Charter did not apply to Germany, was publicly before the whole world showing up his countrymen as people who . . . well, who go back on their word. Why did he take action that must have been so distasteful to him?

The precise reasons have not yet become known. But it is possible to hazard a guess. In 1941, when the Charter was first announced with much dutiful blowing of the press trumpets, the war was going well for Germany. America was not yet involved and the Russian armies were in headlong retreat. It was by no means certain who would win the final victory.

By February 1944, the situation had undergone a great change. It was by this time fairly obvious that the British-American-Russian combination would be victorious. Indeed, this combination was by then politically omnipotent. It could do what it liked and there was no one in the world to say it nay except the enemy, and he would soon be crushed. The year 1943 had been one of inter-allied conferences; Moscow, Cairo, Teheran, again Cairo. At the Teheran Conference of November 1943, plans were unfolded for splitting Germany up into fragments: also for Russia to absorb the eastern part of Poland and for the latter to be compensated at Germany's expense. As these plans were quite inconsistent with the Atlantic Charter, an essential pre-condition of their smooth realisation was the demolition of the precious Charter. Hence presumably the burial service read two months later by Mr. Churchill, in which the words "no question of the Charter . . . banning territorial transference" gave a plain hint that such transferences, in contravention of the Charter, were in contemplation. Thus died the great Churchill-Roosevelt declaration of international rights, assassinated by its own parents. It is interesting to record that the funeral was virtually unattended.

What was left as a war object for Mr. Churchill? There were our previous friends, the extirpation of Nazi tyranny and Prussian militarism. Let us take the former first. What can have made Mr. Churchill so eager for his countrymen to destroy the Nazi tyranny in Germany? The tyranny, as such, was not oppressing the British people. That being so, what business was it of theirs if the Germans liked to live under a tyrannical form of Government? Did not the Atlantic Charter declare that the British "respected the right of all peoples to choose the form of Government under which they will live"? Therefore, if the Germans did not choose to throw off their Nazi tyranny for themselves, why should a lot of Englishmen have to die in throwing it off for them?

Assuming, however, that the forcible suppression of tyrannies in foreign countries was a British duty, how came it that another tyranny was made a partner of the British in that process? The Communist tyranny in Russia was worse than the Nazi tyranny in Germany; the general condition of the Russian people was far inferior to that of the Germans; slave

labour in Russia was on a gigantic scale compared
to anything of the sort in Germany, cruelty was certainly no less than in Germany and is thought by many
to have been much greater. The foul technique of
purges, brutal interrogations leading to "confessions,"
and universal internal espionage was in full swing in
Russia years before Hitler introduced such methods
in Germany, which he probably copied from the Russian exemplar. Yet Mr. Churchill hailed Russia as a
most welcome ally when she was brought into the war.
One tyrant to help beat another. Clearly, tyranny of itself it was no aim of Mr. Churchill's to destroy.

He did not even show much interest in the overthrow of Nazi tyranny itself when a prospect of
achieving it was brought to his notice. The Bishop of
Chichester has recently told how, in Stockholm in
1942, he met two anti-Nazi Germans who asked him
to find out whether the British and American Governments would negotiate for peace with a German democratic government if the Hitler regime were overthrown. The Bishop put the matter to Mr. Eden on his
return, but the British Government made no response.

What of the restoration of independent sovereignty to the countries overrun by Germany, to
which Mr. Churchill had referred in his speech in
the House of Commons on June 18, 1940? All these,
he had said, should be liberated; and especially France,
who should be "restored to her former greatness." In
this latter intention, Mr. Churchill was claiming su-
pernatural powers. France could be freed from German domination by Anglo-American arms. But as to
"greatness," the French might restore that to themselves (if it had lapsed) or the Almighty could do it
for them, but no one else could. Even the Almighty
would have had a hard task, for French greatness was

a thing of bygone times. For years before 1939, France had been rotten with corruption, misgovernment, and general decay, these being the principal causes of her swift collapse in 1940. Actually, Mr. Churchill's formula for France's restoration to greatness was the one that was certain to fail. Had France been compelled to struggle back to her feet by her own efforts, a revival of national health might have been possible. But to have a share in the occupation of Germany and other appurtenances of power and mighty achievement presented to her by other hands was the surest way of pushing her further down the slippery slope.

The other and smaller occupied nations were not promised greatness, but only their freedom, which it was more within Mr. Churchill's capacity to bestow on them. This they duly received. Yet no sooner had they obtained it than Mr. Churchill himself set to work to get it back from them. He became the foremost British, if not European, protagonist of a Federation of Europe, by joining which the smaller "liberated" States would have lost their sovereignty almost as surely as they had lost it to the Germans before the liberation.

But if the unity of Europe was Mr. Churchill's ideal, why was he so remorseless in destroying the European unity that Germany had achieved in 1940? It is true that the German unification of Europe had been by force of arms. But Mr. Churchill, as an historian, should have known that this was the way that nearly all unities had been secured: Italian unity, French unity, German unity, American unity, Spanish unity.

Europe had been unified once before—by Napoleon I. And it has not been everybody who has applauded the destruction of that unification by the

Battle of Waterloo. "It is characteristic of Pitt, who was the chief architect of the (third) Coalition, that he contemplated, when the war was over and victory won, the summoning of a congress to devise a federal system for the maintenance of a European peace. Napoleon, too, had a scheme for reorganising Europe as a Commonwealth of enlightened but unfree peoples under French hegemony; and there are some friends of European unity who still regret the frustration of his dream." *

The Germans, as we know, began with the endeavour to be the irreproachable conquerors. British newspapers in 1940 reported the excellence of their manners in France, German soldiers jumping up in trams and buses to offer their seats to women passengers, and so on. But Mr. Churchill successfully sabotaged that endeavour by encouraging and arming the European resistance movements, largely composed of the Communist underworld, who by guerilla terrorism provoked the Germans into reprisal measures against the civil populations of their occupied countries, and thus wrecked the chances of fraternisation. The German overlords might have been hated and opposed in any case. Who can say? There were undoubtedly appreciable collaborationist movements in all the conquered countries, even in France, and it is possible that collaboration might have prevailed over resistance had not resistance been deliberately organised from abroad with the help of air power.

This is not to say that resistance was not valuable to the anti-German cause. The point is that it was not the unification of Europe which Mr. Churchill was determined to prevent, but only its unification by Germany. It is to this that the "extirpation of Nazi

* Dr. H. A. L. Fisher—*History of Europe,* Vol. III, p. 884.

tyranny" narrows down. From the very early days of the war, this attitude of Mr. Churchill's mind was made manifest; as, for example, when the Germans had invaded Norway and Mr. Churchill said in a speech that "the sacred soil of the Vikings must be cleansed from the foul pollution of the Nazi invaders." I do not recollect him referring to the "foul pollution of the sacred soil of the Letts, Lithuanians, and Esthonians" by the Russian annexer.

We thus appear to be left with the extirpation of "Prussian militarism." The word Prussian is commonly used in England to suggest an aggressive and militaristic outlook. If Mr. Churchill used it in that sense here, he was of course being inaccurate. In fact, the German General Staff, Prussian or otherwise, had on the whole been opposed to the warlike solution of Germany's problems. The man who had insisted on war had been Hitler, and Hitler was an Austrian.* "Austrian militarism" would therefore have been a truer utterance.

However, if we take the "extirpation of Prussian militarism" to mean the complete defeat of Germany, then there is no cause to doubt that this was Mr. Churchill's object. Time after time, in speech after speech, he made it clear that complete victory was his aim. He might or might not, as far as his countrymen could tell while the war was in progress, have had other aims. That he was working for the total overthrow of Germany no one could doubt. The important question therefore arises, was that his only true aim?

He himself can be quoted to show that it was. "You ask," he said in the House of Commons on May 13,

---

* Though Hitler had some Czech blood in his veins and was therefore of partly Slav origin.

1940, just after he had become Prime Minister, "you ask, what is our policy? I will say: It is to wage war, by sea, land, and air, with all our might and with all the strength that God can give us; to wage war against a monstrous tyranny, never surpassed in the dark, lamentable catalogue of human crime. That is our policy. You ask, what is our aim? I can answer in one word: Victory—victory at all costs."

What the politician says in public does not, however, always express his inner intentions. Is there, therefore, any corroborative evidence to confirm that Mr. Churchill's policy and aim, as declared above, represented his real resolve? One who was in close touch with Mr. Churchill during the whole war and was in a position to form a judgment on this point has expressed the opinion that such was the case. General Sir Leslie Hollis, Deputy Chief Staff Officer to Mr. Churchill when Minister of Defence, in a lecture at the Royal United Service Institution on 4 October, 1950, said in answer to a question about the Government's war aims:

"I would say that our war aim was victory, and as far as my knowledge of the subject goes, those who had the direction of affairs said 'Let us have victory first, and then we can get down to war aims.' "

This expression of opinion receives clear support from the description of an interview between Brigadier Fitzroy Maclean and Mr. Churchill before the Brigadier departed for his mission with Marshal Tito during the war.*

". . . there was one point which, it seemed to me, still required clearing up. The years that I had spent in the

* *Eastern Approaches*—Fitzroy Maclean (Cape), p. 281.

Soviet Union made me deeply and lastingly conscious of the expansionist tendencies of international Communism and of its intimate connection with Soviet foreign policy . . . If, as I had been told, the· (Jugoslav) Partisans were under Communist leadership, they might easily be fighting very well for the Allied Cause, but their ultimate aim would undoubtedly be to establish in Jugoslavia a Communist regime closely linked to Moscow. How did His Majesty's Government view such an eventuality? Was it at this stage their policy to obstruct Soviet expansion in the Balkans? If so, my task looked like being a ticklish one.

"Mr. Churchill's reply left me in no doubt as to the answer to my probem. So long, he said, as the whole of western civilisation was threatened by the Nazi menace, we could not afford to let our attention be diverted from the immediate issue by considerations of long-term policy. We were as loyal to our Soviet Allies as we hoped they were to us. My task was simply to find out who was killing the most Germans and suggest means by which we could help them to kill more. Politics must be a secondary consideration."

The case could hardly have been put more plainly. Politics were of minor importance. Long-term views did not count. All that mattered was to kill Germans, to defeat Germany, to achieve which there were "no lengths in violence to which we would not go." On this point, the testimony of Brigadier Maclean is in accord with that of General Hollis.

A British observer in France has reached the same conclusion as myself on this matter. In his book on France during the Occupation, Mr. Sisley Huddleston says:

"On this, then, Churchill and Roosevelt, although they disagreed on many other issues, were in full agreement: the immediate aim was to smash Germany. They were

willing to set everything aside in the pursuit of that objective, and to let tomorrow take care of itself." *

We know from Mr. Churchill himself that Mr.
Huddleston was right about the President. Describing the arrival in England in January 1941 of Mr.
Harry Hopkins, the closest confidant and personal
agent of the President's, Mr. Churchill remarks that:
"there he sat, slim, frail, ill, but absolutely glowing
with refined comprehension of the Cause. It was to
be the defeat, ruin, and slaughter of Hitler, *to the
exclusion of all other purposes, loyalties, and aims.*" †

But if the killing of Germans and the utter defeat
of Germany did, in truth, constitute the real governing object in Mr. Churchill's mind, what, it may be
argued, was wrong with that object? Is not the utter
defeat of the enemy just what one wants to achieve
in war? How, then, could Mr. Churchill have been
mistaken in working for it? Let us examine that point.

* *Pétain, Patriot, or Traitor?* p. 134 (Andrew Dakars). Published in U.S.A.
as *France: The Tragic Years* (Devin-Adair).

† Mr. Churchill, Vol. III, pp. 20 and 21. (My italics.)

8

Mr. Churchill's Mistake

"War," said the Prussian General von Clausewitz a hundred and twenty years ago, "is a continuation of policy by other means." The operative word in that is "policy." War is embarked upon for political purposes, for the furtherance of a policy. The military part of the business, the "other means" of Clausewitz's definition, is ancillary to the political. Countries prefer to achieve their policies towards their neighbours by negotiation and agreement. It is only when the chance of agreement becomes remote that a resort to force is considered, according to whether the particular policy is regarded as sufficiently important to justify the risks of a forcible solution.

The policies which give rise to a decision by violence are of various kinds. The most common are the desire for someone else's territory, someone else's markets, someone else's wealth, or all three; also the urge to spread some gospel, ideological or religious. The desire for territory was behind the German-Polish war. The desire for markets was behind the

Anglo-Spanish wars of the sixteenth and eighteenth centuries, the Anglo-Dutch wars of the seventeenth century, and the American-Japanese war of the twentieth. President Wilson, speaking in 1919, expressed the opinion that all modern wars are of this nature.

"Is there any man or woman," he said, "let me say is there any child, who does not know that the seed of war in the modern world is industrial and commercial rivalry? This was an industrial and commercial war."

It is, however, an ideological crusade, the universal establishment of Communism, that is said to be Russia's permanent object in relation to the rest of the world; though that crusade may, for all I know, have an economic motive behind it. Russia has not yet resorted to "other means" in furtherance of this object, but the present western rearmament programme is based on the assumption that she might.

The point is that war postulates a political reason for going to war, whether offensively or defensively, and therefore a political object to be gained or lost according to how the war goes. Without such a political object, a war becomes meaningless slaughter.

What, then, was Mr. Churchill's political object which his use of force was intended to attain? There is little doubt that the answer must be that he had no such object. His object was victory. But victory is not a political object but a military one. War is, in fact, no more than one course of action for realising a political aim, of which diplomacy is the other. Mr. Churchill's warlike thinking seems to have stopped short at the course of action and not to have gone on to embrace any clear political object to which victory should lead.

Victory can be a legitimate final object for a General, an Admiral, or an Air Marshal, for at that point his function as a warrior ceases to operate and diplomacy resumes full charge of the situation. But it is no final object for the politician. On the contrary, it is for him no more than the milestone where he politely thanks the warrior for his services and proceeds to make the reverse application of Clausewitz's principle of the "continuation of policy by other means," this time substituting negotiation for violence. If the original policy, in support of which resort was had to force, has been clearly thought out and if the victorious politicians have kept their heads during the passions and vicissitudes of the violence, the policy after victory will be approximately the same as the policy before the war commenced.

If, however, a resort to war does not mark a continuation of policy but, instead, an abrupt change of policy from whatever it was in peace time to the achievement of military victory, then the gaining of that victory can only mean the opening of a door on to a political black fog. And since Mr. Churchill seems to have made this abrupt change, it is hardly surprising that the victory he sought at all costs has proved almost entirely sterile. To achieve this victory he was prepared to sacrifice everything, and the sacrifices he did make then left the British co-victors semi-bankrupt, rationed, financially imprisoned in their island concentration camp, their Empire disintegrating, their own country occupied by American troops, and their national economy dependent upon American charity. And what for? That the Germans might be permanently disarmed? Within three or four years, we were begging the Germans to rearm as quickly as they liked!

But if Mr. Churchill pursued the wrong object, based on the false premise that Germany was the butcher-bird of history, how did he come to make that elementary mistake? One cannot tell. But it is very possible that his undeniable zeal for the personal direction of warlike operations may have obscured his political outlook. There is not the least doubt that all his life he has harboured an eager desire to move armies and ships about the globe, and to act as a supreme War Lord. The main cause of his quarrel with Lord Fisher in 1915 was not so much the conflict of opinion about the Dardanelles campaign as his own behaviour in frequently taking the conduct of operations out of the hands of the First Sea Lord and the naval officers and ordering them himself, very often without the Sea Lords being told what was being done until it was an accomplished fact. That Mr. Churchill exhibited exactly the same tendency to collect all the operational strings into his own hands in the Second World War is amply revealed in his own books about that struggle. It may be, therefore, that the politician in Mr. Churchill was sacrificed to the strategist.

Whether it was to make a good or a bad strategist is a matter about which much will inevitably be written in the course of time. It is, however, irrelevant to the present point; which is that, in order to try his hand as a Whitehall Napoleon, Mr. Churchill appears to have neglected his proper function as a Downing Street politician. With his gaze riveted on the mirage of military triumph, he failed signally to appreciate the purpose of such a triumph, if it could be achieved. Failed, that is, or deplorably misjudged the political probabilities which it was his peculiar responsibility to forecast with accuracy. What sort of

peace with Germany was desirable, whether by
complete victory or by negotiation, would depend
on how the international situation was likely to be
influenced by such different military outcomes of the
war and how the various major Powers, both allied
and enemy, could be expected to react thereto.
These reactions it was Mr. Churchill's primary business as a politician to estimate, and his estimates (if
he made any) were dreadfully wrong. He either
allowed himself to believe that, if and after Germany
was crushed, Russia would behave as a model neighbour, or he was persuaded to that belief by President
Roosevelt who, whatever his mental acumen in dealing
with the complexities of American politics, became
during the war an uncritical admirer of Josef Stalin.
Or possibly Mr. Churchill was so immersed in the
multifarious tasks into which he had thrown himself
as the organiser of unconditional victory that he had
no time left in which to wonder what that victory
would be for. Whatever his exact mental processes,
there can be no doubt that in his own proper sphere
as a politician, with the duty of evolving a sound
political object for which the war was being fought,
his failure could hardly have been more complete.

It may be argued that Mr. Churchill could not
have known beforehand that Russia would turn
against the West after the war. The undoubtedly correct answer is that it was his job to know. That was the
very sort of thing that it was his true function, as a wartime political leader, to judge. Just as a general has to
estimate what are the enemy's strategical plans and
devise suitable military measures for bringing those
plans to nought, so has the politician to guess the
political plans of both friends and foes and frame his
own country's policy accordingly, together with the

broad lines of strategy which depend on that policy. In each case, the measure of success is accuracy; and since no excuse is accepted for bad guessing by the general, there is no reason why it should be in the case of the politician. Results are the only test.

The chance of Russia "going sour" on her British and American allies was by no means beyond human imagining. On the contrary, it is the sad record of alliances that their members very often do disagree after victory has been won. Serious differences developed between the British and French within a very short time of the defeat of Germany in 1918. The Balkan allies who were victorious over Turkey in 1912 immediately quarrelled and went to war among themselves. Indeed, brawling over the spoils of war can be said to be more or less proverbial. There were, in fact, not a few people in Britain who had grave doubts about the post-war loyalty of her wartime associates, and some of the doubters voiced their misgivings in public. For instance, Lord Huntington, speaking in the House of Lords on 11 October, 1944, said:

"It is most unlikely that over a term of years, without a threat from an outside enemy, the Big Five should have no quarrel and no dispute. If they do quarrel, who out of them is going to condemn the aggressor? . . . it is unfortunately almost the fact that allies, after a big war, do fall out. During the pressure of this war, we have already seen signs of stresses and strains, and there will be plenty of conflicts lurking in ambuscade for the victors."

Moreover, if any British politician could have been expected to feel uncomfortable about Russia's future reliability, it was surely Mr. Churchill. It was he who had been mainly responsible for the attempt in 1919 to prevent by force of arms the establishment of Communism in Russia, and in 1940 he had been a supporter of the expedition (which actually never started) to aid the Finns against the Russian invaders of their country, at which time Mr. Churchill had made the historic remark that "Communism rots the soul of a nation."

Yet at Yalta he agreed to hundreds of thousands of square miles of Polish (to say nothing of Lithuanian, Latvian, and Esthonian) territory being made over without their inhabitants' consent to the soul-rotters, in flagrant disregard of that Atlantic Charter which he and the President of the United States had trumpeted to the world earlier in the war, and in patent disdain of the British declaration of war against Germany in 1939 in support of the inviolability of Polish territory. In addition, the compensation given to the Poles from east German territory and the allocation of half of the rest of Germany to Russian occupation had the effect of removing the historic buffer between Muscovy and the countries bordering the Atlantic.

There was no realistic reason for placing any trust in Russia's loyalty as an ally. She was fighting on the same side as Britain only because she had been driven into it by the German attack. In the twenty-two years between 1917 and 1939, she had set no new example to the capitalist world of international trustworthiness and straight dealing. Far from it. That Mr. Churchill, for a quarter of a century the foremost critic among British politicians of Communist Russia, could have been blind to the adverse possibilities of the Yalta proposals, and particularly the bisection of Germany to the Russian advantage, is hardly conceivable.

But if he was not, how did he come to accept

demands made by Stalin at Yalta which were so violently inconsistent with Britain's declared reason for entering the war with Germany and which, if Mr. Churchill believed what he had preached from 1917 to 1941, were so obviously ominous with future menace to European stability? It can be argued that Russia would have taken what she wanted in any case, whether Mr. Churchill agreed or not. It can also be admitted that President Roosevelt was by then not only in a state of infatuated hallucination regarding the virgin purity of Marshal Stalin's motives but was desperately anxious to save American lives in the attack on Japan by inducing Russia to come into the Far Eastern War. For this latter purpose, the President was ready to bribe the Russian dictator with Polish and German territory in Europe, though this meant throwing the whole European ethnic and political situation into the melting pot and incidentally making a mockery of the British reason for declaring war in support of Poland in 1939. There is also little doubt that a powerful inducement to both British and American acquiescence in the Russian demands was the dropping of hints by the Russian delegation that, were any serious difficulties raised to their wishes by the British and Americans, they (the Russians) might consider coming to separate terms with Germany.

It might seem that, in the face of all these complications, Mr. Churchill was helpless and could only fall into line. But, in fact, the decisive argument really lay with him, if he cared to use it. If any member of the coalition against Germany were to threaten a transfer to the German side as a means of coercing its associates, that form of pressure need not have been confined to the Russians, who were

by no means ideally placed to exert it. If the Germans
had been presented with a choice between an arrangement with Russia and one with Britain, there
is no doubt they would have leapt at the one with
Britain. For that they would have agreed to almost
any reasonable terms and would have overturned
Hitler and his Nazis without hesitation. Even Hitler
himself had from the very start been only too anxious
for an understanding with Britain, and would have
welcomed it beyond anything. So much is clear from
Captain Liddell Hart's and Mr. Hinsley's books, as
we shall notice again later on.*

If, therefore, there were to be any hints about coming to terms with Germany, Mr. Churchill could
have dropped them the most effectively of any of the
Big Three. It was he, in fact, who held the trump
card in the Anglo-American-Russian triangular game,
by means of which he could have forced the other two
to conform to his will. Why did he not play it; and, by
playing it, avoid the dangerous and distressful situation in which Europe and Britain now find themselves?

Though various reasons could be advanced for
his neglect of this opportunity, there were two dominating considerations that absolutely precluded any
thought of such tactics. One was Mr. Churchill's
supreme object of bringing the Germans to complete
and final defeat. Given his fixed and unswerving adherence to unconditional surrender as his object, his
submission to Russian-American notions about the fate
of Germany became inevitable. Without his allies'
combined help, Mr. Churchill could not defeat Germany and his object could not be achieved. As long,

---

* *The Other Side of the Hill*, by Captain B. S. Liddell Hart (Cassell).
Hitler's Strategy, by F. H. Hinsley (Cambridge Univ. Press).

therefore, as he held to that object, he had no option but to accept his allies' dictation. But had his object been political instead of military, the position would have been quite different and the world might now be in a safer state.

We will now go on to examine the other reason.

9

The High Cost of Hatred

By the time the "Big Three" were assembled at Yalta in 1945, the British people had for nearly six years been subjected to an intensive hatred propaganda against the Germans, in which the latter had been depicted as the embodiments of everything evil. They were declared to be the sole causes of the war; and not only this war but the previous one and most other ones before that. They were held up to obloquy as leading the way in cruelty, duplicity, a ruthless disregard of civilised conventions, and general turpitude. They had, so it was claimed, started the bombing of open cities,* and in their conduct of the war had thrown legality to the winds. Reference has been made in Chapter 2 to the rampant denunciation of everything Germany handed out to the public by such a highly placed man as Sir Robert Vansittart, whose bitter reproaches could reasonably be taken by the man in the street as being based on full knowledge.

* See also pp. 126, 127.

Nor had Mr. Churchill been any less vituperative than his diplomatic lieutenant. From the beginning of the war, and more especially since his accession to the premiership in 1940, he had assailed the Germans with a verbal cannonade of abuse and threats. There was nothing too bad he could say about them. Twice running they had been the criminals who had turned Europe into a slaughterhouse, their present leader was a "bloodthirsty guttersnipe," they themselves must "bleed and burn," and there were "no lengths in violence" to which the British would not go to destroy their wicked power. After years of listening to and reading such sentiments about their principal enemies from their Prime Minister and his host of imitators, the British people had naturally come even before 1945 to regard the Germans as first cousins of the devil. Therefore, for Mr. Churchill to have suddenly come out with an announcement that Britain was dropping out of the war because the Russians and Americans were proposing to treat the Germans too harshly after their defeat, and still more that Britain might join Germany against them, would have struck the British public dumb with a combination of astonishment and horror.

It could not have been done. The population of the British Isles had been worked up by propaganda to a state of passionate hatred of Hitler, the Nazi party, the German Armed Forces, and the German people. They had been told repeatedly that "the only good German was a dead one" and that the unconditional surrender of Germany was the war aim. They could not have tolerated the abrupt abandonment of all these ideas.

Yet their strenuous indoctrination with this hatred of the enemy and the belief that he must be overthrown at all costs stood them in very ill stead when one of their allies took or threatened to take a different attitude towards that enemy. If Stalin could give the impression that he might pull out of the fight against Germany, with a fair prospect of being believed, it obviously gave him a decisive advantage over Mr. Churchill if the latter was irrevocably committed to a German defeat. The whip hand in obtaining what he wanted politically would then be with Stalin, and Mr. Churchill would be obliged to dance to the crack of the Russian whip, however damaging to Britain's long-term interests that dance might be. And in so far as Stalin did obtain this whip hand in securing British agreement to post-war conditions which are the main cause of the present dangerous world tension, it was precisely because his object was political and not purely military; because his vision extended beyond victory to the political prizes to be gained therefrom, and was not narrowed and confined to the victory alone. He saw victory, as Clausewitz did, as a means to an end, and not as an end in itself. The evidence is that Mr. Churchill took the latter and more limited view of warfare, and was therefore helpless against Premier Stalin's more long-sighted purposes.

Stalin, of course, had no need to consider public opinion, which became patriotic or lethally deviationist according to how he and his associates of the Politbureau might change their minds. Besides, after 28 years of strict obedience to a ruthless Governmental opportunism enforced by purge and liquidation, Communists in Russia and all over Europe were well-conditioned to drastic reversals of policy, to eating their words, to denouncing a foreign nation as a set of Fascist hyenas one day and hailing them as fellow-workers for the Red Paradise the next. For the very reason that British public opinion did not possess this convenient pliability, it was elementary wisdom on the part of British wartime politicians to avoid arousing too much popular passion against the German enemy in case reasons of State should later require that enemy to be regarded more benevolently. But Mr. Churchill went out of his way to excite such passion by every means in his power. Everything in this world has its price; and the price of the hatred propaganda so sedulously disseminated among the British people in the Second World War turned out to be a very heavy one, in the shape of an inflamed rigidity of mind about the Germans that left the British an easy prey to their more calculating Russian allies.

The mass of the British people could not be blamed if they responded to hatred propaganda during the war and believed their political leaders when the latter repeatedly said that the only hope for the world was to bring the Germans to complete and utter defeat. The average man had no reason to mistrust the soundness of such advice. The only other big war of his lifetime had ended with just such a German defeat, followed by a dictated peace; and if there were criticisms of that peace in the inter-war period, the loudest and most persistent of them had been to the effect that the German overthrow had been inadequately brought home to the German people and that the Treaty of Versailles was insufficiently harsh. If, therefore, the British man in the street was told after 1939 that the Second World War was due to too great a leniency on the former occasion, why should he doubt it? He had little or no knowledge of the history of warfare, and was therefore unaware that the great majority of major wars in which England had taken part since the Conquest had ended, not in total victory, but in a negotiated compromise peace. In fact, of the fourteen wars that Britain had waged against a white enemy between the days of the Spanish Armada and the German War of 1914, only two, the war against Napoleon and the Boer War, had been carried to complete victory.

Nor, as has already been mentioned in Chapter 2, were any of these fourteen British wars fought against the German "butcher-bird." Nothing of the sort. In the middle seventeenth century, Britain's principal foes were the Dutch. In the late seventeenth century and all through the eighteenth century, the French. Between the overthrow of Napoleon in 1815 to the end of the nineteenth century, our only active white enemies were the Russians and the Boers.

Historically, moreover, there is nothing permanent about alliances. The warlike grouping of the nations, as might be expected, has been under frequent change, to preserve the balance of power or to snatch the advantages of the moment. Thus, Britain was fighting with France against Holland in 1672, but with Holland against France in 1689; or, again, with Russia against France in 1814, and with France against Russia in 1854. It is, indeed, an historical commonplace that the enemy of one war is the ally of the next.

And sometimes, even, the ally of the same war. In 1793, the Spaniards were on the side of the British against the French. In 1796, they changed over the other way and became the allies of the French against the British. In the next (Napoleonic) war, they did the same thing, but in reverse. Initially allied to the French and thereby sharing in the shattering defeat of Trafalgar, in 1808 they threw in their lot with the British against the French and co-operated with Wellington's army in pushing the French out of the Iberian Peninsula.

Russia has a noteworthy record of alternation. In 1798, she joined in the war against the French. Only two years later, she was forming the Armed Neutrality of the North with Sweden and Denmark, directed against Britain. In 1804, after the Peace of Amiens, she participated in the new war against France, but this mood lasted only three years. By 1807, Russia had changed sides again and the Czar had become a warm friend of Napoelon's, concluding secret treaties with him against Britain. By 1811, however, the two Emperors were at loggerheads, and in the following year the Czar was at war with Napoleon. Thus, between 1798 and 1812, Russia had changed sides no less than four times.

These examples of change of front are not historical curiosities of the past. The twentieth century has seen it happening again. In July 1914, Italy was part of the Triple Alliance, the other members of which were Germany and Austria. The stipulation that Italy would be absolved from the obligations of the alliance if England were ranged on the other side allowed her to stand aside from the outbreak of war in the following month. But a year later, she abandoned her neutrality, and entered the war. In favour of her former allies? Not so, but against them. She did the same in 1943 after her capitulation to the Anglo-American invaders of Italy. Again she turned against her German allies. Mr. Churchill apparently saw nothing disgraceful in this reversal of loyalty, but described it as Italy "working her passage" to respectability.

In the summer of 1939, when a conflict between

Britain and Germany was almost a foregone conclusion, Russia was negotiating with both sides at once for an alliance. She chose the German side, undoubtedly because she saw the greatest advantage to herself in so doing.

Mr. Churchill himself was not averse to a British military *volte-face* in the case of France. She and Britain had entered the war as allies, pledged to make no separate peace. However, in 1940 France was driven out of the war by the irresistible factor of defeat in the field. Against that compelling argument no accusation of desertion holds good. *Force majeure* is decisive.

Thereupon, Mr. Churchill sent a naval squadron to demand the surrender of the French ships at Oran (Mers-el-Kebir), failing which they were to be sunk. The surrender was refused, fire was opened, the French battleship *Bretagne* was blown up, and two others driven ashore, at the cost of 1500 French sailors killed. Let the British not deceive themselves into thinking that this was not making war on the French. It fits exactly into Clausewitz's definition of war as "a continuation of policy by other means." The policy was to ensure that the French Oran squadron could in no circumstances be used against the British. It was hoped to arrange for this by negotiations. But when negotiation failed, the "other means" of direct force were employed. This was war.

War was also waged against France in North Africa (the Americans co-operating—being, indeed, in chief command), in the Normandy landing and subsequent operations on French soil, and in the aerial bombings which preceded and accompanied such operations.

It can be argued that the French were longing to be liberated from German occupation and were therefore anxious for an anti-German invasion of France. That they wanted an end to the occupation was natural. But whether they wanted it that way is surely more questionable. We shall never know for certain, because the French nation was not asked its views beforehand. I have an idea, however, that had it been invited to vote on liberation by a landing in France or by a landing in, say, Holland or Schleswig-Holstein, there would have been a large majority in favour of one of the latter.

In Britain, at the time, the people were told that the Anglo-American bombings of French factories and other targets were highly popular in France; that the French so much liked having their houses blown to bits and their relatives and neighbours killed that they would run out into the streets and wave enthusiastically to the bombers who had done the damage. I thought these stories, as I read them, indicated an almost superhuman degree of patriotism on the part of the French. Sisley Huddleston, who was in France during the war, discredits any waving there may have been as quite unrepresentative of general feeling.

"The bombing definitely did harm to the Allied cause . . . one town that I know (in Normandy) had 2,000 inhabitants killed or wounded out of a population of 5,000, and hardly a house was left standing. It is better not to ask the survivors what they think today. Under the official friendship for England and America there is a smouldering sense of injury . . . they (the French) were pained at the idea that there was no way of separating the Germans from the French, and that they were, in fact, if not in intention, lumped together as the enemy to be hurt. . . ."*

I, myself, being in a part of Courseulles on the Normandy coast on D + 1 day was cautioned against walk-

* *"Pétain, Patriot or Traitor"* (Dakers), p. 202.

ing alone in the less busy parts of the small town, as
the French inhabitants were said to be so vindictive
about the manner of their liberation that they were
taking any good opportunity of sniping their liberators.
To bomb a country, to destroy its factories, to flatten
its towns, to kill and injure its citizens is to make war
on that country, whether it is done or alleged to be
done for the benefit of that country or not. We may
have thought we were doing the French a good turn by
knocking them and their country about. It is undeniable that we believed we were looking after our own
interests at the same time, and it is unlikely that unless we and the Americans had been satisfied on that
latter point we should have indulged in any killing of
Frenchmen for their own good. The time may come,
who knows, when the British may find themselves in a
similar position to the French, and after being atom
bombed by one side may be atom bombed by the
other. Should that happen, I know at least one Englishman who will find it difficult to regard either bombing as the friendly action of a peace-loving well-wisher.

With numerous precedents to support him, and
provided he had taken the precaution of keeping public opinion wisely temperate about the enemy, there
was no reason why Mr. Churchill need have been
squeamish about considering an arrangement with
Germany *if it was to Britain's benefit to make it.* As
the Russians had taken that very line in 1939, and
were known to have been ready to take it again after
1941, it was no striking display of diplomatic finesse
for the British Prime Minister to leave so immensely
powerful a means of moral coercion in their hands
without making any attempt to counter it in kind. To
fail to do so was to make an entirely gratuitous present to the Russians of a bargaining advantage of incal-

culable value. But by 1945 Mr. Churchill could not
help himself. He had thrown so much fuel into the
furnace of anti-German hatred in the previous war
years that the national passion was too fierce to be opposed and Mr. Churchill could only run before the
storm of his own creation. But there is no evidence that
he had any other desire.

Not that hatred propaganda was an invention of
Mr. Churchill's. He was but carrying on the process
which, though as old as warfare, had received a tremendous boost in the previous war of 1914-18. In that
war, hatred propaganda was for the first time given
something like organised attention. The result was a
campaign conducted with huge success and almost
complete lack of scruple. Any distortion or suppression was practised if it could help to blacken the enemy's character. Any atrocity story, whether true or
not, was bruited far and wide; and the stories were
frequently untrue. The utmost publicity was given to
a gruesome report in 1917 that the Germans were boiling down the bodies of their own dead to produce glyc-
erine and other by-products for the manufacture of mu-
nitions. The story made a deep impression on millions
of people in Britain, who were horrified at such ghoul-
ish bestiality and concluded that the Germans were
beyond words evil.

The story was a lie. It was a calculated lie, made up
with malicious intent on the British side and passed
out into circulation with the deliberate purpose of increasing popular passion against the German enemy.
After the war, a British Cabinet Minister publicly confessed as much.*

The hatred campaign of the second war was there-

---

* The Foreign Secretary in Parliament on Dec. 2, 1925. (See Hansard for
that date.)

fore only a continuation of the same policy as had been followed in the first, though it was greatly furthered by the availability of new media. By 1939, broadcasting could bring the hiss of verbal detestation, uttered by practised orators, direct into millions of homes, while the films subtly introduced animus against the enemy into the crowded assemblies of the people's favourite halls of relaxation. The results were all that could be wished by the organisers. Today, eight years after the end of the second German war, there is plenty of evidence that the minds of many of the British are still poisoned by wrath purposely engendered in their wartime hearts against the Germans.

A special cause of British resentment is the memory of the German bombing of London and other cities, immense propaganda capital having been made during the war over the utter German villainy in thus 'starting' the aerial bombing of open towns. It is therefore somewhat startling to read in a book written by an ex-high official of the Air Ministry that not only was it Britain that originated the bombing of civilian targets but that the British should be proud of having done so. To quote the author:

"Because we were doubtful about the psychological effect of propagandist distortion of the truth that it was we who started the strategic bombing offensive, we have shrunk from giving our great decision of May 11th, 1940, the publicity it deserves. That surely was a mistake, it was a splendid decision." *

It may or may not have been a splendid decision. What, however, was unquestionably of masterly skill was the accompanying decision that because we were

---

* *Bombing Vindicated* by J. M. Spaight, C.B., C.B.E., formerly Principal Assistant Secretary at the Air Ministry (Geoffrey Bles).

nervous about enemy "distortion" of our initiative in the matter, we would therefore do the distorting ourselves and put the responsibility on to the Germans.

"There was no certainty," says Mr. Spaight, "but there was a reasonable probability that our capital and our industrial centres would not have been attacked if we had continued to refrain from attacking those of Germany."

Therefore, he adds, our British decision to take the lead in such attacks enabled us to "look Kiev, Kharkov, Stalingrad, and Sebastopol in the face." The further question arises, however, whether our strenuous campaign of false propaganda that the Germans had begun the whole dirty business leaves us in a good position to look our former enemy in the face.

That the feeling of the British populace against an enemy could be relatively free of venom is shown by an episode of 1801. For eight years, Britain had been at war with France. The original outbreak had been largely caused by English indignation at the early excesses of the French Revolution, and particularly the Reign of Terror and the execution of the French King and Queen. During the war that followed, British spokesmen had fulminated against French wickedness, cruelty, and moral obliquity quite as fiercely as their successors did against the Germans of a hundred-odd years later.

But these fulminations did not reach the people in the same way that they have done in this twentieth century. In the 1790s there were no cinemas, no broadcasting, and no popular newspapers to influence the mass of the people with inflammatory headlines and leading articles. In the days before national education, the bulk of the people could not read. Hence,

in those late eighteenth century days the mass mind
could only be reached by local word of mouth, which
put a severe limit on the extent to which popular
opinion could be influenced at all.

The meagre scope for propaganda was strikingly
shown when the Peace of Amiens was concluded between Britain and France in 1801. For when a French
Ambassador returned to England, the London crowd
was so delighted to see him arrive as the symbol of restored peace and had been so little affected by the rancour expressed against the French in educated circles
that it took the horses out of the shafts of the ambassa-
dorial carriage and dragged it enthusiastically to the
Embassy. One simply cannot credit anything of that
sort happening to a returning von Ribbentrop's con-
veyance, in view of the orgy of vilification of his country and countrymen indulged in by the British of
1939-1945, had a compromise peace been made with
Germany in the latter year.

It seems a fair assumption, therefore, that if we
nowadays get more violently excited against an enemy
it is not because we are necessarily more vicious and
vindictive than our forebears of a century and a half
ago, but because as a nation we are better educated and
so succumb more readily to the propagandist. The latter, of course, addresses himself to his task the more
zealously where his patients are more responsive to the
treatment; and is encouraged in his efforts by the politicians, presumably because they believe that hatred
helps the war effort. Superficially, no doubt it does.
But a more measured view may suggest that the deliberate injection of hatred into the general population
is as dangerous as an addiction to drugs on the part of
the individual in creating a psychological craving for
continued indulgence and a morbid rejection of all

moderating influences that might stand in the way; resulting in a war policy determined more by insensate emotion than by cool-headed and practical judgment. It was in keeping with the induced detestation of the chief enemy with which, as never before, the Britain of the Second World War was pulsating, that her leader's war aims were ultra-extremist and entirely scornful of the principle favoured by the Russian and Austrian Emperors in their struggle against Napoleon in 1813, that "the way should never be closed against peaceful tendencies even in the hottest fight." Unconditional surrender was a war policy from which every drop of moderation had been squeezed, and in which the scientific use of calculated restraint could have no place.

10

Politicians in Control
of War

But, it will doubtless be objected, was not the last war the most scientific one that Britain had ever waged? Were not the scientists, indeed, directly associated with war for the first time in our history? On the material side of things, yes, certainly. More destructive weapons, more cunning instruments, more skilful analysis of results were among the scientists' contributions to warfare. But on the moral and psychological side, the last war was the least scientific for a thousand years. As fast as the physical scientists came in at the front door, the human scientists went out at the back.

What, then, is the scientific way of conducting war? In those suspect places, the Service Staff Colleges, where the professionals of warfare, the officers of the Navy, Army, and Air Force, meet to study and discuss their main job in life, certain principles regarding the conduct of war are held to be axiomatic. One of the chief of these relates to the object. It is agreed and stressed that a correct selection of the object is of the first importance, dominating all other factors. As the pre-war Field Service Regulations said, "in the conduct of war as a whole, and in every operation of war, it is essential to decide upon and clearly to define the object which the use of force is intended to attain." Unless you know exactly what you want to achieve, it is a toss-up whether you achieve anything useful; and you may easily exhaust your energy without achieving anything at all.

Nor can the selection of the right object be taken as at all an easy task, but is one that usually requires a lot of hard thinking. The Field Service Regulations give two conditions that need to be observed in choosing the object. First, that it must of itself be capable of achievement; and, second, that even if it is, there must be enough force available to achieve it. Again quoting the Regulations: "The selection of a correct object demands knowledge and judgment to ensure that the resources which can be made available are sufficient for its attainment, and that the results of successful attainment are those calculated in the circumstances to be most effective."

It could well be thought that politicians would never be so stupid as to make war in pursuit of an unattainable object. But any such assumption would be much too optimistic. Take the case of the First World War. The British object in declaring war on Germany in 1914 was officially proclaimed to be the honouring of the British guarantee of Belgian neutrality. But we know that Sir Edward Grey meant to support France against Germany, whether Belgium were invaded or not; and when the suggestion was made by two Field-Marshals, Lord Roberts and Sir John French, at a Cabinet meeting on the day after the declaration, that the British Expeditionary Force should be sent to

Belgium to push the Germans out, it was hastily brushed aside. Sir Edward Grey had already committed the British Army to go elsewhere.

It would seem from the Foreign Secretary's memoirs that direct support of the French had been promised mainly, as we have noted in Chapter 1, to save Britain from "being hated, despised and discredited" for having stood aside.* If, as is said of him, Sir Edward Grey was a bird-lover and knew a lot about the habits of birds, he evidently knew little about the habits of men. It is not the nation which stands aside in war that is unpopular but the one that comes in. From the moment the British became allies of the French in 1914, the French concern was no longer to be pleasant to them but to bully them into doing more. Sir John French had hardly arrived with his army in France when he was treated with extraordinary rudeness by the French General Lanrezac, by General Joffre, by almost every French General he met. By the end of six weeks, he was reduced to a state of bitter indignation. "Never throughout my career," he said, "have I suffered such humiliation; and I have had to come to France to fight for the French for it to be inflicted. I will never forget it." As for the French press, it spent most of the war indulging in the sarcasm that the British were "fighting to the last Frenchman."

Similar tendencies were manifested in the Second World War. Even between the English-speaking Anglo-American Allies, there were important in-

* Indeed, in his post-war book Grey is quite definite on this point. "The real reason for going into the war," he there said, "was that if we did not stand by France and stand up for Belgium against this aggression we should be isolated, discredited and hated; and there would be before us nothing but a miserable and ignoble future." (Lord Grey, *Twenty-five years*, Vol. II, page 15.)

stances of a serious lack of fellow-feeling between comrades in arms. The American Admiral King made no secret of his dislike of the British Navy and preferred to accept avoidable American mistakes rather than to profit by previous British experience. And General Bradley's book on the war has little that is pleasant to say about British generalship and much that is not.

In Britain, there is more tendency to take an interest in an ex-enemy General like Rommel than in any allied officer, American or Russian. Even the allied Supreme Commander, General Eisenhower, now President, does not evoke the same curiosity as the one-time head of the German Afrika Korps.

The explanation of these seemingly strange phenomena is simple enough. Nations fighting on the same side are competitors for honour and glory, and therefore have an interest in belittling the contribution of their allies. It is quite different with the enemy. The more formidable he was, the greater the merit in his defeat. Moreover, all the personal friction of war, in the shape of wranglings and differences of opinion about plans and operations which so often give rise to irritation and rancour, is necessarily between those on the same side and not between enemies. Least likely of all is serious animosity to be shown by belligerents towards neutrals, owing to the latter's usually strong bargaining position as a supplier of belligerent needs and as a potential ally of the future. Sir Edward Grey apparently quite failed to appreciate the nature of wartime relationships, with the result that his reasons for getting his country entangled with France were so mistaken as to have the opposite effect of what was intended and expected.

Another and more recent example of the intrin-

sically unattainable object was Mr. Churchill's proclaimed determination to "extirpate Nazi tyranny"
for all time. It has previously been argued that this
was not the Prime Minister's main object, which is
much more likely to have been victory in the field.
But in so far as Mr. Churchill was harbouring the extirpation idea, he can be said to have been seeking
the unattainable, certainly if he expected to do the
extirpating by brute force. It was an unattainable
intention for this reason, that although you can kill
men's bodies by shells, bombs and bayonets, you cannot shell or bomb or bayonet thoughts out of people's
minds as long as they remain alive. The only sure way
of curing the German people of an addiction to tyrannical government (if it was necessary for the British
to take on that job) was to convince them that Nazi
tyranny did them no good. But that was going to be a
difficult business. The Germans had tried full Parliamentary democracy after their defeat in 1918,
and all it had come to offer them was the prospect of
permanent subjection to a French hegemony in Europe. Disappointed and disgusted, they had then tried
a tyranny; and from the German point of view it had
worked wonders. Within a matter of three or four
years, it had lifted Germany out of the international
gutter and put her back on her feet. There was therefore good reason why the bulk of German people
should approve of and believe in Nazi tyranny, especially as they could see other similar tyrannies produc-
ing correspondingly striking results in Russia and Italy.
Those who had done most to bring Nazi tyranny into
being, as candid spokesmen in Britain, including Mr.
Lloyd George, were ready to admit, were the British,
French and American Governments who had reduced
Germany to despair while under the democratic sys-

tem. The last thing, therefore, that Mr. Churchill's threat to extirpate Nazi tyranny would be likely to do would be to convince the Germans that such tyranny was bad for them. On the contrary, they would regard it as so successful that Germany's foes were determined to destroy it.

And if Mr. Churchill could not convince the Germans that the Nazi system was bad, his declared intention of destroying that system "for all time" was bound to fail. He might be able to drive it underground, as the natural desire of the American people to drink alcoholic liquors was driven underground by prohibition, and as proscribed religions are so driven by persecution. But he could not extirpate it.

The very extremity of the measures adopted after 1945 to root out Nazism were well calculated to ruin any real chance of doing so. It is one of the safest of political prophecies that the hanging of the leading Nazis after the spectacular Nuremberg trials and the drastically inquisitorial campaign of denazification against the lesser Party members will succeed mainly in turning many thousands of former Nazis into future national heroes. It is common knowledge today that a vigorous neo-Nazi movement is simmering just below the surface of German political life. As for the Fascist counterpart of Nazism, the *Times* of 12 May, 1952, reported that the former Deputy Secretary-General of the old Italian Fascist Party had just addressed a crowd of 50,000 sympathisers in Rome itself.

Attempts to carry out Mr. Churchill's idea of suppressing another nation's political system against its will tend, indeed, to be self-defeating; the very fact that a different orthodoxy is sought to be imposed by foreign enemies rendering it automatically obnoxious to those marked down for forcible reformation. It is therefore a God-send to revolutionaries such as the French Jacobins and the Russian Bolsheviks when foreign nations intervene and endeavour to crush out their revolutionary principles by military force. Intervention of this kind materially assisted the success of both the French and Russian revolutions, just as the clamorous ideological hostility of British left-wing extremists towards the Franco régime in Spain did the Caudillo a very good turn by rallying support for him in his own country.

Given enough force and ruthless enough measures, an alien system can be imposed on another country. But when the force is relaxed, as sooner or later it probably will be, the natural national preferences of the people will reassert themselves unless there has been racial fusion of conquered and conquerors. Even after a century of Russian domination, the Poles hated Russian rule; while the Irish dislike of British Government burnt with a white-hot flame after 400 years.

Mr. Chamberlain and Lord Halifax committed the other kind of error in relation to the object in 1939. Their plan of preserving the integrity of Poland was quite feasible, provided they had the military strength to support it. But this they had not got. Britain and France being cut off from direct access to Poland, the only way they could help her in a Polish-German war was by an offensive in the west. The French, however, were not so inclined. They would not fight an offensive war but only a defensive one. And if the French would not attack, the British could not either, being far too weak by themselves. The Western allies therefore sat back inactive while Poland was overrun. Mr. Chamberlain and Lord Halifax had taken on a job so much beyond the resources at their disposal that they made no attempt to carry it out.

Whether they knew, when they gave Poland that guarantee, that the French would take no offensive action in the event of war, I do not know. Though the French General Gamelin was full of boastful optimism in 1938, Sir Eric Phipps, the British Ambassador in Paris, was reporting at the same time that "all that was best in France was opposed to war and that there was a general feeling of defeatism in the country." * But Phipps' opinion may itself have been set aside as defeatist in British official circles. If, however, the British Prime Minister and Foreign Secretary did know that the French would not take the offensive, then the guarantee they gave to Poland was pure bluff, not worth the paper it was written on if the bluff was called; and the Ministers concerned were promising something which they must have known they could not perform. Britain, in that case, was in the position of a bankrupt guaranteeing someone's overdraft.

If they did not know, then they ought to have known; it being their obvious duty to make sure of their ground before promising anything. Maybe the French agreed to an offensive against Germany beforehand but defaulted on the agreement when the time came.† If that was what happened, the French default would not absolve the British Ministers from blame. Men whose duties ordinarily involve dealing with assurances from other people are commonly expected, whether they be bank managers or Foreign

* Transill, *Back Door to War* (Regnery) p. 420.

† It was evidently clear to Mr. Churchill in August 1939 that the French were unlikely to take the offensive. See his Vol. I, p. 300.

Secretaries, to possess the judgment necessary to gauge the worth of those assurances.

It is possible that Mr. Chamberlain and Lord Halifax were influenced towards, if not pushed into, the Polish guarantee by pressure from President Roosevelt in Washington. Professor Tansill, whose very important book, *Back Door to War,* on the origins of the war was published in 1952, quotes evidence to show that Roosevelt was using every channel of approach to urge Chamberlain into war with Germany.* Tansill also indicates that Roosevelt, as well as inciting the British and French to war, was letting them think that the United States would come at once to their aid if and when they should become involved. Thus, Ambassador Kennedy "repeatedly told Chamberlain that America would rush to the assistance of Britain and France in the event of unprovoked aggression," and Ambassador Bullitt in Paris appears to have been saying the same thing.†

The guarantee does not, however, become any more justifiable on that basis. American troops, even if the United States had entered the war "within the hour," could not have reached Europe in time to save Poland. Mr. Chamberlain's pledge to the Poles therefore remains a signal example of an object impossible of realisation for lack of means.

When Mr. Churchill became Prime Minister in 1940 he succeeded to a political object that lay in ruins. He did not replace it by another, but adopted instead a military object, victory through the complete defeat of Germany. This, too, was at this time an object incapable of achievement through lack of means. It is true that Mr. Churchill kept up the pre-

* Tansill, Chapter XXIII.

† Tansill, pp. 450 & 451.

tence that it could be achieved, as when he told the Americans that if they would provide Britain with the tools she would "finish the job." But, in fact, Britain had no hope of finishing the job by herself, and the fact that Mr. Churchill did not really believe that she could do so is sufficiently indicated by his outbursts of thankfulness when first Russia and then the United States entered the war. On the latter occasion, Mr. Churchill declared that:

"This is the object that I have dreamed of, aimed at *and worked for;* and now it has come to pass."

The immensity of Mr. Churchill's relief at the American involvement is plainly indicated by the extraordinary indiscretion of the words I have put in italics. The American nation was known to be traditionally sensitive about foreign entanglements and had an even longer tradition of dislike of the British. American mothers had very recently been assured by their President "again and again and again" that their boys would not be sent to fight in Europe during the war in progress there. Therefore, by volunteering the information that he had "worked for" the entry of the United States into the war Mr. Churchill was going out of his way to invite the accusation among anti-British elements in the United States that the British Government had in some way or other helped to bring about the Japanese attack on Pearl Harbor.

A man does not "work for" the participation of another nation in a war if he thinks his own country can achieve its object unaided. The American Admiral King tried hard to prevent the British fleet taking part in the Pacific naval war because he evidently thought the American fleet could do the job alone, and he wanted all the credit for his own navy.

Mr. Churchill joined a Government in 1939 committed to fight for an object it lacked the resources to achieve. When that Government fell and he himself became Prime Minister, he formulated a new object which could not be attained with the resources available. It could only be realised by the gaining of new allies, the acquisition of which would mean turning a comparatively localised conflict into a world war. Mr. Churchill was vouchsafed those new allies, and the world war came with them.

If the foregoing suggests, as I fancy it does, that modern politicians are not very clever at handling warfare, there need be no cause for surprise in that. Successful war demands the closest fidelity to the facts. Successful politics hinge to a great extent on the verbal manipulation of facts for the benefit of the voting-paper. The habits of mind acquired in political life are therefore no natural qualification for successful war direction and may well be a serious handicap thereto.

Any idea, therefore, that a politician can turn easily from the shadow-boxing of the debating-chamber to the efficient control of the tough and un-usual business of warfare is to be regarded as delu-sive. There is, indeed, no new activity in the world to which mankind seems able to bring a finished skill. Quite the opposite. Nature, for purposes of its own, evidently sees to it that we approach the unaccus-tomed with a sure instinct for doing it wrong. Even the simple process of hitting a ball over a net or along the ground has to be laboriously learnt from an expert if it is to be done with efficiency; and unless thus taught the right way to do it, most people go on play-ing fifth-rate tennis or golf all their lives. It commonly needs a wholetime specialist to be in the forefront of any profession or business. War is an intermittent activity and does not offer a lifetime of continuous experience even to those who become professional warriors; and it is recognised that service officers themselves must put in hard study at Staff Colleges and similar establishments as a necessary complement to practical experience. Even the great Napoleon, who was engaged in active warfare for more than twenty years, did not regard actual campaigning as sufficient for a high commander. The aspirant to superior leadership, he said,

"must read again and again the campaigns of Hannibal, Caesar, Gustavus Adolphus, Turenne, Eugene, and Frederick. Model yourself upon them. That is the only means of becoming a great Captain and of acquiring the secret of the art of war."

Hence, the chances of a politician, whose stock literature is more likely to be social and economic than military, assuming successfully the role of Great Captain at a moment's notice are obviously not promising. Even in militaristic Germany, the politician Adolf Hitler, though some of his political judgments amounted to genius, made a terrible mess of German strategy; and had he left it to his generals, the outcome of the war would probably have been different.

Least promising are the chances for a politician in England, where the public attitude towards warfare is so very peculiar. The inhabitants of the British Isles are a warlike lot who make excellent fighting men when the need arises. The need, moreover, often does seem to arise. Though the English, whose

historical memory is about three years, are convinced that they are amongst the foremost lovers of
peace and are equally certain that the Germans are
the world's principal warmakers, the hard truth was
revealed in the earlier chapters of this book that in
the century before the First World War the British
were at war more often than anyone else.

But in spite of all this abundant experience,
which should make them more knowledgeable on
warlike matters and more war-conscious than all
other peoples, it is a curious fact that in between
their wars the only attitude the general population
of Britain will take towards warfare is to ignore it,
and abuse it if it cannot be ignored. Though no one
dares, of course, to speak slightingly of the rank and
file of the services, civilian speakers and writers seldom, in normally peaceful times, refer to the officers
except in terms of faint derision or active dislike. For
years and years the British Colonel was lampooned
in a London paper as a goodnatured but hopeless
idiot, the embodiment of general fatuity. Financially, the armed forces are treated as unskilled la-
bourers, the chairmen of the new nationalised indus-
tries receiving more than double the pay of the
heads of the services such as the First Sea Lord, and
the Chiefs of the General and Air Staffs. At the Nuremberg trials, the leading British lawyers were
paid fees for 10 months' work that corresponded to
three years' salary for the Service Commanders-in-
Chief whose victories made the trials possible.

In peacetime politics, a reputation for a knowledge of war is a severe drawback, inspiring accusations of "militarism" or "war-mongering." As I write,
the Secretary of State for War, who happens to hold
what I am possibly rash enough to regard as the honour-

able rank of Brigadier, has cast it off in order to call himself plain Mister, with the object presumably of avoiding the odious taint of having been one of the national defenders. That his renunciatory action was hardly the brightest encouragement to his fellow-citizens to join the army of which he was the political head at a time of brisk rearmament shows clearly the depth of his alarm at being thought a soldier in politics.

With the foregoing combination of influences affecting the national attitude to war, it is hardly to be wondered at that a real understanding of warfare and what it means is almost non-existent among the bulk of the British population. Referring to his experiences as a soldier in the South African War, Sir Patrick Hastings wrote:

"I had not the slightest idea what I was fighting about. I wondered (on the way home) if the ordinary man who stayed behind in England possessed any more idea than I did as to what I had been fighting for. Now I am older, I am quite sure he had not."*

And if the British as a nation are almost without ideas on the subject of how to conduct a war, it would not be very surprising if their political leaders were little better. It is not only dangerous for these latter to evince any interest in war during times of peace. In time of war they can count on being able to blunder along on the basis of amateurish trial and error without fear of informed criticism on any scale. Mr. Churchill has himself confessed that the politician does not bring an instructed understanding to the task of war direction. Writing of his share in the

* Sir Patrick Hastings—*Autobiography*, p. 51 (Heinemann).

Dakar fiasco of 1940, he has said, "We were all in our wartime infancy."

Actually, Mr. Churchill's entry into the Cabinet as First Lord of the Admiralty in September 1939, and his succession to the Premiership in 1940, had been popular in the country on precisely the opposite assumption that he had proved himself a master of strategy in the previous war of 1914-18. But if Mr. Churchill himself says no, we can leave it at that. Dakar, after all, was not his first failure in the 1939 war. He had been given Ministerial charge of the Norwegian operations in April 1940, and they had developed into one of the most disastrous muddles of British military history; so disastrous that Mr. Chamberlain, the Prime Minister, was driven from office in consequence.

11

Errors by Wartime Politicians

A judicious selection of an appropriate and attainable object is of the utmost importance in war. It is the essential starting point for the whole subsequent course of warlike plans, operations, and the use of force generally. The object should therefore resemble a lighthouse, built solidly on sound foundations after careful thought as to the best place to put it in order to guide the ship of State safely into the harbour it wishes to make. If, however, it resembles a will-o'-the-wisp, the State is more than likely to fetch up on the rocks. The wars of this century have demonstrated that British politicians are poor judges of what the national object in war should be, with the result, as all men can now see, that the ship Britannia is pounding heavily on the reef. The masts have already fallen, half the provisions have been jettisoned to lighten the ship, and the unhappy crew are living on reduced rations and in daily uncertainty whether the ship can be dragged back into deep water or will go to pieces un-

der their feet. This sorry state of affairs is due very
largely to the misdirection of two wars through the
failure of unskilful politicians, from Sir Edward Grey
onwards, to understand what they were aiming at,
and through their allowing themselves to become
mesmerised by the word "victory." Their misjudg-
ment in this matter is concisely epitomised in a remark made by Mr. Churchill to the House of Commons on June 18, 1940, when he said:

"During the first four years of the last war the Allies
experienced nothing but disaster and disappointment. . . .
we repeatedly asked ourselves the question 'How are we
going to win?' and no one was ever able to answer it with
much precision."

There we have the whole trouble in a nutshell. It
is no wonder that no one was able to answer that
question of "How are we going to win?" *with much
precision,* for the word "win" in this context was itself
lacking seriously in precision. What did "win"
mean? Did it mean destroy the German fleet? Or did
it mean seize the German colonies? Or drive the Germans out of Belgium? Or break up the Austrian Empire, or what? As used by Mr. Churchill it probably
meant victory in the field. We have noted earlier in this
book that he evidently viewed the war of 1939-1945
from the standpoint of military victory and little else,
and it now looks from his above-quoted remark as if
the Cabinet of 1914-18 were doing the same thing.
But military victory, as we have seen, is not or
should not be an end in itself, but is only a means to
an end. If, therefore, the politicians of the two world
wars had not got beyond aiming at the military defeat of the enemy, they cannot have realised that

their proper function was to ask themselves the vastly more important question, "What is our political object?" The next stage in our investigation is therefore to enquire into what that object should have been.

The best approach to this may be to decide first what the political object should not have been. There are certain objects, to which politicians show a marked partiality, which can be classified as bad ones, to be avoided on all occasions. They include political abstractions such as freedom, justice and democracy; or, to put it the other way round, the suppression of tyranny, injustice, and autocracy.

It is one thing for nations to fight to defend their own freedom, system of justice, or democratic form of government. In that case, the best description of their political object in so doing is the word security; security to order their national life in their own way. "Crusades" to bring freedom, justice, or democracy into other nations' lives are quite a different matter. Such crusades have a bad case history. The war to "make the world safe for democracy" of 1914-18 was not a success. In Russia, the Duma, or Parliament, was scrapped and a ruthless dictatorship set up even while the war for democracy was in progress. In Italy, dictatorship sent democracy packing within four years of the end of the democratic crusade, while Germany followed suit not very long after, and Portugal and Spain also joined the authoritarian ranks.

It is not only with individuals that one man's meat is another man's poison, reluctant though politicians are to recognise the fact. Having obviously failed to appreciate from the developments of the inter-war period that the accident of being victorious is no

sound reason for changing the loser's political sys-
tems to conform with one's own, the British politicians of the Second World War declared it to be their
intention to destroy the German dictatorship and to
"re-educate" the Germans in the ways of parliamentary democracy; which, though it may be suited to
the British and the Americans, had never made
much appeal in Germany, has for years been a bad
joke in France, and has now been banished altogether from the whole of eastern Europe except
Greece. Even in England professorial voices are being
raised to predict that parliamentary government is on
its last legs. Moreover, as we saw in the last chapter,
the endeavour to impose a political system on a defeated enemy by force is quite enough by itself to make
that enemy throw it off at the first opportunity.

The other crusading aspect of the 1914-18 war,
"the war to end war," was a worse failure than its
democratic companion. The armistice of 1918 was
not a year old before the British and French were
fighting the Bolsheviks in Russia in the vain attempt
to stifle the Communist regime at birth. In the following year (1920), the Bolsheviks were invading
Poland. In 1921, the British and Irish were locked
in bitter strife. In 1922, came the Greco-Turkish
war, and in 1923 the French invaded the Ruhr.
About 1924 began the long-drawn-out struggles of
the various war lords in China; in 1931, the Japanese
occupied Manchuria and, in 1932, attacked the
Chinese at Shanghai. In 1935, the Italians were at
war with Abyssinia; in 1936 the Spanish Civil War
broke out; in 1937 the Japanese began their war
against China; and in 1938 the Germans marched
into Austria, in 1939 into Czechoslovakia, and in
the same year into Poland. But the Second World

War that came with the last-named event had hardly
begun when British politicians started afresh to
speak hopefully of permanent peace if only their
fellow-countrymen would fight hard enough to overcome the German enemy—as they had said on the
previous occasion.

There is little enough hope for crusades to make
the world more virtuous, and none at all if they are
conducted with unlimited violence and the abandonment of all civilised restraints. The obliteration
and atom bombing of open cities and the arming and
encouragement of the midnight cut-throats of the
underworld masquerading as "resistance movements" are not calculated to inculcate Christian
righteousness in mankind. The world is now in a more
disturbed and lawless state than it has been for centuries, perhaps than ever before. There is cold war in
Europe, hot war in Korea, trouble in Persia and
Egypt, brigandage in Malaya, insurrection in Indo-
China, Mau-Mau terrorism in East Africa, racial
rioting in South Africa, anxiety everywhere. In Britain, crimes of violence increased alarmingly after
1945, and have not even yet, eight years later, been
got under proper control; while the prisons of the
country are crammed to two or three times their
designed capacity. In France, M. Jean Giono, the
well-known author, told Mr. Warwick Charlton, who
was investigating the atrocious Drummond murders
on behalf of "Picture Post":

"During the war and during the liberation the people of
the country, who were normally law-abiding and kind,
in appearance at least, became beasts: women are known
to have torn young boys who could have been their sons
into pieces with their bare hands. And a young man I

know, who seems quite harmless, after raping a woman, poked her eyes out, cut off her ears, and otherwise mutilated her with a kitchen knife. His excuse was that she spoke with a German accent. She was in fact a French woman from Alsace." *

The British Government's wartime boast of its intention to bring freedom, to the enslaved German people has been a complete failure. All that has happened is that arbitrary government by the Nazi party has been exchanged for arbitrary government by foreign High Commissioners, under whom politically unpopular newspapers are suppressed and politically suspect individuals are summarily arrested and imprisoned just as they were between 1933 and 1939. And should the foreign occupation forces be withdrawn, there would obviously be nothing to prevent a new form of internal despotism being established at once, should the Germans so wish; as the partitioned, despoiled, and weakened state of their country following on Yalta and Potsdam might well make them wish.

It is, moreover, unpleasantly characteristic of crusades that the crusaders seem prone to adopt the very abuses which they go to war to suppress in other people. Thus, the crusade to restore freedom to Germany led to British freedoms being suspended right and left. Freedom of speech was interfered with in order to "prevent the spread of alarm and despondency," and the liberty of the subject was savaged by the 18B Regulation which allowed men and women to be cast into prison without charge or trial and kept there at the Home Secretary's pleasure, being

---

* "Picture Post," 11th October, 1952. What a story this would have made at Nuremberg had it been done by a German.

denied all legal assistance. All that was necessary was that the Minister should "have reasonable cause to believe" that the detention was desirable in the public interest. There was thus created in Britain a direct counterpart of those German concentration camps which had been so bitterly assailed by British politicians and publicists. These two forms of tyranny reacted on each other, and it became quite a common occurrence for Members of Parliament, who spoke under the protection of privilege, to demand the summary incarceration of anyone who dared to express views that they disliked and could represent as in any way unpatriotic or which could be construed as damaging to the war effort.

Six years of suppression of 'dangerous thoughts' have left their mark on the British people, who nowadays display a noticeable timidity in giving that free expression to their opinions on current, and especially international, affairs which would have been taken for granted at the beginning of the century. "Freedom is in peril," said the official posters of 1939, "defend it with all your might." These posters spoke the truth but not all the truth. Freedom was in peril not only from outside the country but from inside it, too.

Indeed, the conduct of the war by the democracies themselves was hardly an inspiring example of democracy in practice. The two chief democratic leaders, President Roosevelt and Mr. Churchill, went about the world to top-level conferences where they made Olympian decisions as to how the war was to be fought and how the world was to be carved up after it, how many hundreds of thousands of square miles of territory were to be taken from one country and given to another, and how many millions of wretched refugees were to be driven from their homes in consequence.

The war had to be got on with, and it was clearly impracticable for top-level conferences which involved long journeys by the President of the United States and the Prime Minister of England to be reconvened, perhaps more than once, because objections were raised in Parliament or Congress. But other methods could have been used. If the conferring had been done on a lower level by ambassadors or even Foreign Secretaries, the home Cabinets and Parliaments could have exercised some control over what was agreed. As it was, the decisions reached by the highest men clearly had to be forced through the democratic legislatures as *faits accomplis.* Thus we find Mr. Churchill, after Yalta, brusquely disposing of Parliamentary criticism by saying that the Soviet leaders were "honourable and trustworthy men" and that he "declined absolutely to embark here on a discussion about Russian good faith." *

Such high-handed procedure cannot be called democratic. Nor can it be justified by the argument that the Prime Minister knew best and that his estimate of the situation was the right one. We know that, in fact, he was disastrously wrong. "The impression I brought back from the Crimea," Mr. Churchill told the Commons, "and from all other contacts is that Marshal Stalin and the Soviet leaders wish to live in honourable friendship and equality with the western democracies. I know of no Government which stands to its obligations even in its own despite more solidly than the Russian Soviet Government." * This must surely rank as one of

* *The Times,* February 28, 1945.

the most serious political misjudgments in history.

This danger attending Big Three decisions was not overlooked in America, where Mr. W. R. Burgess, speaking on behalf of the American Bankers' Association, told the Banking and Currency Committee of the U. S. House of Representatives on March 21, 1945, that:

"The negotiation of international agreements is a double task. They must be negotiated with the representatives of foreign countries; they must also be negotiated with our people at home. It is all too easy to forget the second step . . . to make an agreement abroad and then to hope to sell it at home. But selling is not negotiation."

Freedom, justice, civilised conduct and democratic self-government are exceedingly tender plants that grow well only in conditions of peace and order. War, so far from stimulating them, causes them to wilt and wither. "No one could expect Parliamentary democracy," said the London *Times* on May 31st, 1952, "to flourish among all the horrors, chaos, and devastation of the (Korean) war that began two years ago."

The radical unwisdom of fighting for abstract principles is emphasised by the completely negative results of the "finest hour" of 1940. If that was, as Mr. Churchill has it, a period of great glory for Britain by which she put the rest of the non-Axis world in her moral debt, the payment of that debt is long in coming. So far from being treated with honour and respect by other nations for her valiant stand in 1940, Britain has received an unheard-of series of slights, rebuffs, and injuries since 1945. The Albanians mined British warships. The Argentines sent gunboats to seize British islands in the Falklands group. The United States has been rubbing in Britain's reduced status in the world by demanding and obtaining all the supreme commands of all the U.N. and N.A.T.O. forces. Even Britain's ancient pride, her Navy, is now for the most part taking its orders from American Admirals; so much so that the British Admiral commanding the coast of (British) Scotland gets his appointment from the other side of the Atlantic. The Indians were so forgetful of the "finest hour" that they took the earliest postwar opportunity to get rid of the British who had governed their country for two centuries. In the Middle East, the heroes of 1940 have received one kick in the face after another; first from the Jews in Palestine, then from the Persians, shortly afterwards from the Egyptians, and then from the Iraqis. In Persia, the finest-hourers were hustled roughly out of their own huge oil properties with threats and imprecations and a loss of £300 millions.

But if there are so many unsound reasons for going to war, what are the sound ones? Again, the Field Service Regulations come to our aid. A nation goes to war, they say, "to protect its vital interests." Not, be it noted, to protect another nation's vital interests. It is a point very much to be noted, because democratic politicians frequently overlook it. Judging from their utterances over recent years, many of the British variety believe that British armies should range the world setting other people free from their brutal oppressors— the Czechs (1938) and the Poles (1939) from the wicked Germans, the Finns (1940) from the wicked Russians, the Greeks (1941) from the wicked Germans, the wicked Germans themselves (1940-1945) from the even wickeder Nazi regime, the Spaniards (1945 onwards) from the wicked Franco, and the

South Koreans (1950) from their former fellow-countrymen across the artificial frontier of the 38th parallel of latitude.

Mr. Churchill must clearly be included in this company. Mr. Stettinius records him as saying to President Roosevelt at Yalta that:

"There were many countries on the face of the globe at the present moment where the populations were in fear of their own Governments. People must be freed from such fear, and he (Mr. Churchill) concluded his point dramatically by saying: 'As long as blood flows from (sic) my veins, I will stand for this.' " *

The word "duty" was frequently on Mr. Churchill's lips during the war and nearly always it referred to Britain's duty to aid someone else. Indeed, I have come across no instance, at any rate after the fall of France, when Mr. Churchill stated it to be some other nation's duty to come to the aid of Britain. Whenever such an act of assistance did occur, it was a "magnificent piece of generosity" or "the most unsordid deed in history" on the other nation's part. But from his speeches, generosity or unselfishness does not seem to have entered, after 1940, into Britain's support of others. It was just her duty.

Take the case of the Far East early in 1942. In a speech on 27 January, Mr. Churchill declared that:

"Our duty is to pass reinforcements of every kind, especially air, into the new war zone, from every quarter and by every means, with the utmost speed."

The "new war zone" was the south-east Asia inter-allied command *after Singapore had fallen*, and therefore *after* the principal British interest in that region

* *Roosevelt and the Russians*—W. R. Stettinius, p. 72.

has passed into enemy hands. But in the very same speech, Mr. Churchill made it clear that it had also been Britain's duty not to take the necessary precautions *beforehand* to ensure that Singapore and Malaya were not lost to the Japanese.

"It would evidently have been very improvident use of our limited resources if we had kept large masses of troops and equipment spread about the immense areas of the Pacific or in India, Burma, and Malay Peninsula, standing idle, month by month, year by year, without any war occurring.* Thus we should have failed in our engagements to Russia. . . ."

The above can only mean that in Mr. Churchill's view it was wrong to use warlike forces for the preservation of British interests in the shape of British territory, and right to use it for the benefit of Russia. Mr. Churchill had, of course, got the matter the wrong way round. Britain had no treaty obligations towards Russia and therefore could not have failed in her engagements to that country. A much more pertinent question is whether she had failed in her engagements to the British Empire.

A British politician who promises British armed assistance to another country is offering the lives of an unknown number of his fellow-citizens to that country, an offer that he has no right to make except for the very clear and definite good of the community to which those citizens belong. He has no right to make this promise merely because he disapproves of Nazism or Communism or some other -ism in some

---

* Yet, eleven months before, in February, 1941, Mr. Churchill had referred in a letter to General Wavell to "the increasingly menacing attitude of Japan and the plain possibility she may attack us in the near future."

part of the world, or hates the Germans or the Japanese and likes the French and the Chinese, or entertains any other combination of prejudices and preferences; or even because an influential section of his political supporters share his likes and dislikes. The only proper test of an offer involving the conditional sacrifice of British lives is whether purely British interests are advanced or likely to be advanced thereby. Queen Victoria had this principle firmly in mind. "She will never, if she can prevent it," she wrote, "allow [Britain] to be involved in a war in which no British interests are involved"; and she defeated an attempt by Lord Palmerston to act otherwise.

British politicians and private citizens are, of course, perfectly free to harbour what personal partialities and passions they please about the ways of the foreigner. But unless their own country's vital interests are unequivocally affected by the situation in another land, their only honourable course, if they wish to strike a blow against Fascism in Italy or Sovietism in Russia, or whatever it may be, is to go there and strike it themselves.

The duty of a country is, in fact, primarily to itself. And the duty of a politician is to his own country, the country which pays his salary. This is a proposition that politicians seem often to have difficulty in keeping in mind. We have seen in Chapter 1 how Sir Edward Grey was considerably influenced in committing Britain to war by his fears of what foreigners might think of him if he did not. Indeed, British politicians of this century seem to be curiously subject to an inverted sense of loyalty which makes them more anxious to please foreigners than their own people. In the First War, Mr. Lloyd George

intrigued continuously and with final success to get
the British armies in France put under French command. In the Second War, they were first put under
French and later under American command. Mr.
Chamberlain handed over the British declaration of
war against Germany to the Polish Government:
Mr. Churchill the declaration of war against Japan
to the American ("within the hour"). Mr. Aneurin
Bevan even went so far as to propose that British
generals in command of British armies should be
replaced by Poles, Czechs, or other refugee officers.
And, after the war, Mr. Attlee agreed to put the bulk
of the British Navy under American command,
against the published protest of the most distinguished British Admiral alive.

Mr. Churchill manifested a very cosmopolitan view
of his responsibilities during the war. His advent
to the Premiership in 1940 was generally approved
in the country because people believed he understood war and was the best politician to rescue them
from the sorry plight in which they then were. There
can, however, be no doubt that what the British
people chiefly expected of him was that he should
preserve British independence against its destruction by the enemy. I say the enemy, because it cannot
have crossed the minds of the people that their independence would be in jeopardy from any other
quarter, least of all from Mr. Churchill himself. They
could not have guessed that he would endeavour to
shatter the 900-year-old separate sovereignty of the
British Islanders by making an offer of common citi-
zenship to the French.

There is not a shadow of doubt that, in making
this offer, Mr. Churchill was exceeding his duty and
his mandate. His own comments on the episode in

his book are very instructive.* The project does not
appear to have originated either in the Cabinet or
Parliament or with the Chiefs of Staff, but came from
a scratch lot of individuals which included Sir Robert Vansittart, Major Morton,† then acting as Personal
Assistant to the Prime Minister, two Frenchmen in
London on an Economic Mission, and General de
Gaulle; none of whom possessed any political authority. When the matter came to be considered by
the Cabinet, Mr. Churchill records how surprised he
was to "see the staid, solid, experienced politicians
of all parties engage themselves so passionately in
an immense design whose implications and consequences were not in any way thought out. I did
not resist but yielded easily to these generous surges
which carried our resolves to a very high level of
unselfish and undaunted action." This charming passage must not be allowed to obscure the fact that
generous surges and high levels of unselfishness were
entirely out of place on this vital occasion. The one
and only criterion that should have governed the
deliberations of those staid, sober, and experienced
politicians was the interests of their own country.
Those and nothing else. And if generous surges arising
out of their heart-throbs for bleeding France really did
dictate their attitude towards the proposed Anglo-
French union, they were being wholly forgetful of
their principal duty of looking after the British.

They seem to have suffered the same functional
'black-out' in respect to Mr. Churchill's contempo-
raneous message to President Roosevelt about the
British fleet. "The present Government and I," he
signalled on 15 June, 1940, "would never fail to send

* *Second World War,* Vol. II, page 180.

† Now Sir Desmond Morton.

the fleet across the Atlantic if resistance was beaten down here. . . ." This assurance by the Prime Minister of England to the head of a neutral state all too plainly reveals that his Cabinet did not understand its position and responsibilities. It was the national trustee for the best use of the armed forces to defeat the foe. If it could not defeat the foe, it had failed in its task as trustee and it was implicit in the trusteeship that it should admit its failure and consult the nation as to what to do next. The fleet was not the Cabinet's own property to do with as it liked in the event of defeat. The fleet belonged to the nation which had paid for it; and if the nation could have got better terms for itself from a hypothetical German conqueror by surrendering the fleet to the enemy, it was undoubtedly entitled to surrender it, the Cabinet's views on the subject notwithstanding.

A point of this kind is of much more than academic interest, because it involves questions of fundamental and overwhelmingly important principle. Had the British fleet gone to Canada or America, the British people remaining in Britain would have lost all control over its future use. It might have been employed in all sorts of ways of which they would not have approved. It might have been used to blockade and starve out a German-occupied Britain. It might even have helped to bombard the coasts of Britain in support of an American landing, just as it was used to bombard the coasts of formerly friendly France in the Normandy and Riviera landings of 1944.

The British people should make up their minds while there is time whether they wish their own weapons to be turned against themselves in such a manner as is thus envisaged. The author found it highly ominous to be told not long ago by a man high up in the publicity services of the country that it might in certain circumstances be the duty of Britain to be bombarded, bombed, starved and devastated "for the greater good of humanity." So far as the author is concerned, humanity can get its greater good in some other way. He would derive no comfort from the fact that Tibetans, Texans, Persians or Peruvians were living in greater security because London had been reduced to powder by atom bombs dropped by British-made, if not British-manned, aircraft. The words duty, loyalty, and responsibility, in their political contexts, seem to have become almost hidden by the sands of ambiguity, perhaps intentionally. When a man like Chiang Kai-shek, claiming to be a patriot, demands that his country should be bombed by the United Nations in order to kindle revolts against his political opponents, the average person throughout the world can feel grave concern about the texture of the modern politician's patriotism.*

If, therefore, we can eliminate other nations' vital interests as a reason for asking one's fellow Britons to shed their blood on the battlefield, and if we agree that this sacrifice can properly only be called for in support of the vital interests of their own country alone, the question still remains what those vital interests are. There is no precise answer to that question, an exact definition being to some extent dependent upon the circumstances of the particular case. Here, however, is the answer provided by Sir Edward Grigg, now Lord Altrincham, in a book he published just before the war† at a time when people were exercised in their minds as to why we

* "Daily Telegraph" of 1st July, 1952.

† *Britain Looks at Germany*, p. 35.

should go to war with the Germans, if we did. The chief material British interests, he then said,

"include, of course, the defence of British territory, the expansion of British trade and the security of British investments."

The defence of British territory does, indeed, seem a self-evident reason for going to war. Self-respecting nations do not care to have their property filched without putting up a fight—if they feel they can. The Dutch evidently felt it was hopeless to fight for the retention of their Indonesian possessions in view of the barely concealed encouragement of the rebels by the United States. The British Government, to the astonishment of many Englishmen, evidently felt itself unable to fight for the retention of the immensely valuable property of the Anglo-Iranian Company at Abadan. Whether the Governmental decision to scuttle out without a blow struck was due to fear of Russia or to the embarrassment of a nationalising Socialist Government in Britain at the thought of opposing the nationalisation of the British-owned Persian oil industry by the Persians, or to some other cause, is not yet publicly known. These recent episodes are nevertheless exceptions to the historic rule that sovereign nations do not allow themselves to be dispossessed without an endeavour, even if a hopeless endeavour, to dispute the act of brigandage; and it is a curious thing that although the British Government was not prepared to fight for the British oil industry in Persia it was ready to send British soldiers to their deaths in order to defend South Koreans against their brethren from the north.

Where, however, actual subjugation is involved,

nations can generally be relied upon, even in these strange days, to defend themselves. "Gallant little Belgium" was applauded for doing so in 1914, as was Finland for standing up to Russia in 1940.* It is superfluous to argue whether such a decision by any country is strategically sound, it being commonly accepted that in such an emergency it is pride and honour that are the paramount considerations.

Assuming that a country does intend to take up arms against a threat of foreign attack, it has two ways of doing so. It can wait until the attack develops or is obviously on the point of developing and then take counter-action; which need not, of course, be confined to the defensive. Or it can anticipate eventual attack by making the first move itself, this latter being given the name of a preventive war. The argument for waging such a war is that it enables a country to meet at its own selected moment a challenge it believes must develop sooner or later, instead of leaving that favourable choice to the other side.

Recent history suggests, however, that the advantage to be derived from preventive action is illusory. The Austrian declaration of war against Serbia in 1914 and the British declaration of war against Germany in 1939 were both of a preventive nature. Austria hoped to frustrate Serbian ambitions against the Austrian Empire by striking first. But this preventive action did not save her Empire. Similarly, Britain feared a German attack at a time of Hitler's choosing, after he had dealt 'one by one' with his other victims. The British preventive war on behalf of Poland did not, however, prevent just this German attack from being made; and although Britain was

* The Czechs were an exception.

able to defeat it, she would have been strategically even better equipped to do so had she awaited without trying to forestall it. And the same applies, as we saw in Chapter 1, even more cogently to the conditions of 1914.

A preventive war has, moreover, the great moral disadvantage that it involves the appearance of an aggressive role. Austria, and with her Germany, lost much in adverse world opinion from this cause in 1914. And although it has often been proclaimed that Germany started the 1939 war, there are not a few Englishmen who are uncomfortably aware in their hearts that the British declaration of war against Germany before any hostile act had taken place against distinctively British interests was not an unequivocally defensive action. The French managed much more skilfully in 1914, when, although willingly committed to a Russian forcing of the pace that was bound to lead to war, they succeeded in presenting themselves before the world as models of defensive hesitation to open fire.

A preventive war also implies a certain confession of defeat. It means that your nerves are not strong enough to stand the strain of the cold war any longer. The British guarantee to Poland was an open admission of such defeat, being mainly designed to quiet the palpitations of the home population; or perhaps one ought to say the House of Commons. Similar displays of neurosis have manifested themselves over the Korean war, periodic agitations having taken place among public men both in the United States and Britain to bring anti-Communist matters to a head by dropping atom bombs on Peking and even on Moscow.

To rush into a preventive war is not only to risk the

accusation of aggression, as with Austria in 1914. It is to prejudge an issue which has not yet arisen and which, if left alone, might never arise. The more we know about Hitler, the less certain it is that he intended ever to attack England or would have done so unless provoked. Indeed, Captain Liddell Hart has produced evidence of first-class importance to the effect that Hitler would probably not have attacked Britain had Britain refrained from going to war with him. In his account of his conversations with the German generals when prisoners of war in Britain, which he published under the title of *The Other Side of the Hill,* Liddell Hart relates how Blumentritt told him that Hitler intervened in the operations at the time of Dunkirk in such a way as to ensure that the British army should get away to England. The German generals in charge were dumbfounded and outraged at Hitler's attitude in thus preventing them from pressing an advantage which they believed would result in the capture of the whole British Expeditionary Force. But Hitler was adamant in his refusal and issued the most peremptory orders for the German forces to be kept at a distance while the British embarkation went on. And he gave the reasons for his apparently lunatic conduct. To quote Blumentritt:

"He then astonished us by speaking with admiration of the British Empire, of the necessity for its existence and of the civilisation that Britain had brought into the world. . . . He compared the British Empire with the Catholic Church—saying they were both essential elements of stability in the world. He said that all he wanted from Britain was that she should acknowledge Germany's position on the Continent. The return of Germany's lost colonies would be desirable but not essential, and he would even offer to support Britain with troops, if she should be involved in any difficulties anywhere. He concluded by saying that his aim was to make peace with Britain, on a basis that she would regard compatible with her honour to accept."

This amazing revelation of Hitler's views about Britain cannot be disposed of as war propaganda used for deceitful ends. It was obviously not propaganda at all but a private expression of policy to Hitler's own generals, the genuineness of which receives the strongest support from the operational orders that accompanied it and which cannot have pleased the officers receiving them. It must therefore be taken as a definite possibility, if not probability, that Hitler would not have attacked a neutral Britain in any case and that the frequently expressed fear by British public men that he had the Island Kingdom on his list of intended victims was baseless. Therefore, unless Blumentritt's testimony can be disproved, we are brought face to face with the staggering conclusion that the British declaration of war in 1939 may have been based on a false assumption of the worst kind. And if Hitler did not really want to subjugate Britain, the larger accusation against him of planning the domination of the world must be even more unlikely.

The expansion of trade and the security of overseas investments are in a different category. Being material factors themselves, their status as warlike objects is logically to be governed by material considerations. The expansion of trade has often been a cause of Britain going to war, one occasion when this was openly so being the second Dutch war in the seventeenth century, Monck telling the assembled Council of State which was debating the situation,

"What matters this or that reason? What we want is the carrying trade the Dutch now have."

The expansion of trade being essentially a business matter, a possible war for that purpose needs to be regarded from a strictly business point of view. If the economic advantage to be gained from the increased trade resulting from the contemplated war is greater than its estimated cost, then the war will be worth while; otherwise, it will not. To what extent trade entered into the British decisions to make war on Germany in 1914 and 1939, I cannot tell. There are those who believe that it was fear of German trade competition on both occasions that played the major part in taking Britain into war with her most serious trade rival. If this was so, the decisions were both of them commercially unsound. The expense of each of these wars to Britain was so enormous that it is unlikely that German trade undercutting could have done Britain's economic position anything like as much harm.

Similar arguments apply to overseas investments. It has been estimated that before the First World War Britain possessed overseas investments worth £8,000 millions, and was the richest nation in the world. If the security of those investments was the cause of the two anti-German wars, those wars might as well not have been fought, for the cost to Britain of the two victories over Germany caused the huge total of her former investments to be completely dissipated.

The two world wars demonstrated the questionable wisdom of expecting to smash important rivals by war. The unconditional surrenders of both Germany and Japan in 1945 gave the victors exceptional opportunities to retard their late enemies' recovery by the dismantling of competitive factories and by other administrative action. Yet today, after only eight years, the economic recuperation of both the defeated countries is so far advanced as to be causing grave apprehension in British business and government circles. Moreover, the process of beating down German and Japanese trade rivalry by war has led to other trade rivals reaping a rich harvest at Britain's expense.

War can, in fact, be a poor and unintelligent remedy for another nation's trade competition. As a rule, such competition is dangerous mainly because the competitor nation works harder than you do. The true solution is therefore for you to work harder than he does; or, as an alternative, to come to some cartel arrangement with him. To use war for stifling his enterprise has the inherent defect that, if defeated, he will then have the powerful psychological incentive to work even harder to put his ruined and subjugated country back on to its feet, while your own people will, as the victors, expect to sit back and enjoy the fruits of victory by taking things easy.

There have, it is true, been occasions when it has paid Britain to go to war for economic reasons. Her nineteenth-century world trading position was the outcome of two centuries of war for overseas markets against the endeavours of the Spaniards and the Dutch to keep them close preserves of their own, and for the control of the North American continent and India against the similar ambitions of the French.

But if these British wars were commercially justifiable, it is most important to note that they were all distinguished by the common characteristic of being economically waged. They were conducted as wars of limited effort for a specific object, and were terminated, like Bismarck's wars against Denmark and Austria, when that object had been obtained. In the seventeenth and eighteenth centuries, Britain fought her wars by using her sea power to the full and eschewing great efforts on land. She won India and Canada and South Africa on the oceans, and therefore cheaply. Though she did not in those times entirely refuse participation in land warfare, her efforts there were essentially diversionary to her amphibious thrusts and were conducted mainly by subsidies to allies and by the employment of foreign, chiefly German, troops rather than by British armies which, when employed, were relatively small. Even in the great struggle against the French Revolution and Napoleon, Britain as usual relied principally on her sea power and was more often than not an onlooker while French armies marched victoriously across Europe. As G. M. Trevelyan has said:

"After our expulsion from the Netherlands in 1794, it is true that we stayed in the war when others submitted to France, but we kept our armies out of Europe for a dozen years together, safe behind the shield of the Navy. We took no serious part, except naval and financial, in the wars of the two coalitions that suffered defeat at Marengo and Austerlitz. Nor, until the Peninsula War of 1808, did we begin to fight on land as a principal, and even then with armies of not more than 30,000 British at a time . . ." *

Even at Waterloo, as we noticed in Chapter 2, only just over 20,000 British troops were engaged.

It was not until the twentieth century that, mainly due to Sir Edward Grey, we threw over our well-established practice of fighting our wars on the sound business principle of getting the largest profit

* *History of England*—G. M. Trevelyan, p. 572.

for the least expenditure, and plunged into unlimited warfare, aiming at complete victory without counting the cost. We did the same in the war of 1939, the slogan for which was "total war."

12

The British Object in 1815 and 1945

Who invented the term "total war" I do not know. In my recollection, it came into vogue after Hitler's advent to power in Germany and was accepted uncritically by the mass of the British people, the meaning commonly attached to it being that twentieth century war was (for reasons unexplained) something entirely novel which had to be waged to the death by the whole conscripted resources, human and material, of the country. Mr. Churchill certainly seems to have subscribed to the idea and to have done his best to translate it into action. To repeat his words: "There is no sacrifice we will not make and no lengths in violence to which we will not go." Nor was this any idle statement. Mr. Churchill showed by his conduct of the war that he was a strategical totalitarian seeking complete conquest at any price instead of pursuing a carefully thought out and calculated national advantage to be gained, to quote another phrase from the Field Service Regulations, with a due regard for "economy of force." We know also that President Roosevelt was of the same mind. As Mr. Churchill told the Commons on his return from his visit to the President early in 1942: "When we parted, he wrung my hand, saying, 'Fight this through to the bitter end, whatever the cost may be.'"

Yet it is not at all obvious why the war of 1939 should have had to be any more 'total' than the war against Napoleon or against Louis XIV or against Philip II of Spain. The British islanders of the Hitler period had no cause to suppose that their national safety was any more precious to them than it had been to their predecessors of Pitt's time or Marlborough's or Drake's, or that their skins were more valuable. Why, then, should this so-called total war be considered essential in the twentieth century when its necessity had not occurred to the British of the eighteenth, seventeenth, and sixteenth?

As a matter of fact, the 1939 war did not start on a total basis. Mr. Chamberlain, the Prime Minister at its outset, had set a definite limit to violence. Whatever the lengths, he said, to which other belligerents might go, the British Government would never resort to the deliberate air bombing of civilian targets. Much the same limitation applied to ground bombardment, and the instructions given to General Mackesy for the Norwegian campaign included the injunction, recorded by Mr. Churchill in his first volume, that "it is clearly illegal to bombard a populated area in the hope of hitting a legitimate target which is known to be in the area but which cannot be precisely located and identified" *; a statement which, if true, clearly makes most of the later bombing of Germany also illegal.

* Churchill, Vol. I, p. 482.

Mr. Chamberlain's "untotal" views on warfare lasted, however, no longer than his own premiership. No sooner was Mr. Churchill in the saddle than such limitations were cast aside. Believing that "bombers alone could provide the means of victory," * Mr. Churchill instituted the bombing of civilian targets without reserve, although this complete change of policy was for a time suitably camouflaged. By 1942, however, there was no longer any serious pretence that civilians were not being attacked. The Chief of Bomber Command, Air Chief Marshal Sir Arthur Harris, told the Germans by broadcast that he was bombing their homes; while the new term "area bombing" then being introduced to describe British bombing policy was in patent disregard of the spirit of General Mackesy's instructions just referred to. Mr. Churchill himself left no room for doubt about his utter rejection of his predecessor's attitude to civilian bombing. "I may say," he said, "that as the year advances, German cities, harbours, and centres of production will be subjected to an ordeal the like of which has never been experienced by a country in continuity, severity, and magnitude." † Total war was on.

Nevertheless, the concentrated and devastating air attack that Mr. Churchill directed against the German cities and people did not bring the victory by bombing in which he had put his faith. Terrible as was the punishment inflicted on the German population and enormous as was the damage and destruction to German cities and towns, amounting to a major blow at European civilisation, Germany fought on.

* Churchill, Vol. II, p. 405.

† Hansard for 2nd June, 1942.

Not only fought on, but her military means of doing so did not seem to be seriously affected. German war production went up instead of down. According to the United States Strategic Bombing Survey, the output of German aircraft, tanks, and many other forms of war material in 1943 was higher than in 1942. In 1944, the output was higher than in 1943: and it continued to rise throughout 1944. When it eventually fell, it was mainly due to Germany being overrun by hostile armies.

Strategic bombers as a means of bringing victory were a remarkable failure, and in a double sense. Not only did they not have the effect Mr. Churchill expected of them, but the very high priority accorded to bombers in Britain's scheme of war production inevitably meant the starving of the other arms and weapons of war, which all went short to a greater or lesser extent in order that a huge national effort to turn out thousands and thousands of bombers should not be impeded.* The adverse effect of the consequential delays was particularly felt in relation to coastal aircraft, so important in the war against the U-boats, and to landing craft and amphibious equipment, so essential for the deployment of military force against the enemy. By allowing these and most other elements of a balanced war effort to be neglected for the benefit of one special weapon designed for direct attack on the enemy civil population, Mr. Churchill made a strategical error of the first magnitude, which good judges estimate to have prolonged the war, perhaps by as much as a year.

Historically, the direct attack on the civil objective

---

* In the debate on the Army Estimates in March, 1944, the Secretary of State for war stated that more labour was employed on making heavy bombers than on the whole of army equipment. *Hansard*, Mar. 2, 1944.

without the prior defeat of the enemy's armed forces has never come off.* Such direct attack being the simplest form of war, we can be reasonably sure, humanity being what it is, that had it also been the most successful form no other would ever have been heard of. It is a tenable assumption, therefore, that because it came to be recognised over the ages that the overthrow of the enemy's organised fighting forces and not the slaughter of his women and children was the most efficient way of conducting warfare, such slaughter was eventually frowned on by the Western nations. "Civilised" warfare was not only more civilised but gave better results. We had a wonderful opportunity in the last war of combining virtue with good strategy, but we threw it away. It is worth a moment's thought whether the enthusiasts for the atom bomb as a weapon of mass slaughter should be allowed to jettison the next opportunity.

Mr. Churchill's—and President Roosevelt's—conception of total war was not confined to strategy but extended to victory and the post-victory treatment of the enemy. Victory had to be complete: surrender unconditional. Similarly, the enemy was not merely to be defeated. His government was to be destroyed, his armed forces abolished, and his country occupied and held down for a generation or more. With these, too, there has been disappointment and disillusion. Unconditional surrender, though achieved, has been widely condemned as a serious mistake, while the total subjection of the German enemy has had to be hurriedly relaxed in order to meet a new emergency which that very subjection had brought about.

It is very significant that the war leaders of a cen-

---

* The Japanese armed forces had already been defeated when the atom bomb was dropped.

tury and a half ago showed no inclination for the concepts of total war, total victory, and total subjugation of the enemy. In those earlier days, the men who decided such things were mostly aristocrats; in England Members of Parliament by personal right and with no need (Parliamentary representation being then largely a preserve of the upper classes) to consider the prejudices and emotions of a mass electorate whose ignorance of foreign affairs and of the full issues of war and peace must always be greater than its knowledge.

The British statesmen who had conducted the war against Napoleon took a noticeably moderate view of warfare. They did not talk of the enemy "bleeding and burning"; they did not acclaim the business of "killing Frenchmen" as desirable in itself; and they did not openly threaten the enemy's civilian population with annihilation, as was done in connection with "obliteration bombing." Nelson admitted to hating the French. Nevertheless, his last prayer, written with the enemy in sight, contained the hope that "humanity after victory would be the predominant feature in the British fleet."

Nor did Wellington speak of "crushing French militarism for all time," though he had just as good an excuse for such a sentiment as Mr. Churchill had in relation to the Germans of the twentieth century. On the contrary, the Duke went out of his way to urge that French militarism should not be crushed at all. He emphasised how essential it was that precisely the opposite should happen; that the French should be treated with the utmost leniency, in order that they might retain their self-respect and be deprived of any sense of grievance. And the reason the Iron Duke gave for this advice in his despatches to Lord Castlereagh, the Foreign Secretary, is very perti-

nent to the peace-making problems of 1918 and the
present day. Leniency to the conquered, he affirmed,
was essential to the peace and tranquillity of Europe.
There were those who at that time wished to deal
with France as Germany was dealt with a century
later. The soldier who had done more to lay France
open to this treatment than any other of his countrymen would have none of this. France was defeated
and helpless and could have been carved up and
weakened according to the victors' will: which, had
it been done, would have, of course, been carried
out in the name of peace and security. But Wellington was wholly opposed to any such dismemberment
of the fallen enemy. It would not, he declared, make
for peace at all.

"There is no statesman who . . . with the knowledge that
the justice of the demand of a great cession from France
under existing circumstances is at least doubtful and that
the cession would be made against the inclination of the
Sovereign and all descriptions of people, would venture
to recommend to his Sovereign to consider himself at peace
and to place his armies on a peace establishment. We must,
on the contrary, if we take this large cession, consider the
operations of the war as deferred till France shall find a
suitable opportunity of endeavouring to regain what she
has lost; and, after having wasted our resources in the maintenance of overgrown military establishments in time of
peace, we shall find how little useful the cessions we have
acquired will be against a national effort to regain them.
In my opinion, then, we ought to continue to keep our
great object, the genuine peace and tranquillity of the
world, in our view, and shape our arrangement so as to
provide for it. . . . If the policy of the united Powers of
Europe is to weaken France, let them do so in reality." But
"if peace and tranquillity for a few years is their object,

they must make *an arrangement which will suit the interests of all parties to it and of which the justice and ex-
pediency will be so evident that they will tend to carry it
into execution."* *

In the light of the very different attitude taken
towards the German enemy in our own day, these
views of the Duke's deserve the closest scrutiny. It
will be observed that he makes no call for the abolition of war or the disarming of the enemy nation and
expresses no hope for or expectation of the everlast-
ing peace which has been so popular a political
slogan in this twentieth century since 1918. The
cautious aspiration to "peace for a few years" is the
most that this soldier-statesman will allow himself.
To reach even this limited goal, he condemns the
tempting principle of the spoils to the victors. He
realises that for the *genuine* peace and tranquillity
of the world, which he regards not only as his
country's "great object" but also the primary need
of Europe, it is not sufficient to coerce the former troublemaker. France's co-operation must be
obtained; which can be secured only by a peace
which will "suit the interests of all parties to it,"
and which the defeated French as well as the victorious British, Austrians, Prussians and Russians
will feel to be just and reasonable.

It was this co-operation of the late enemy, this
pampering (as it would undoubtedly be called nowadays), that Wellington and Castlereagh worked
for at the Congress of Vienna, both of them declaring
that their task was "not to collect trophies but to
bring back peace to Europe"; an aim for which
they received the full support of Count Metternich,

* Wellington's Despatches, XII, p. 596. Present author's italics.

the Austrian Chancellor. The result was a provi-
sional settlement in which pampering was predominant and punishment almost entirely absent. Nor
was "liberation" on the victors' list. France was not
only to be left intact, but was to retain certain of
her European conquests. The bulk of her lost colonial
territories were to be restored to her. The art
treasures "collected" during her years of conquest
were to remain with her. And there was to be no war
indemnity. There can be no doubt that the statesmen
assembled at Vienna were dominated, under the
British and Austrian leadership, by the desire for
"peace and tranquility" before all else.

They were unquestionably aided in adhering to
this attitude by the presence at the conference table
of a French representative on equal terms. Talleyrand was an adroit negotiator and took the obvious
course, for him, of endeavouring, and with success,
to play off one section of the victorious Powers against
another. But that he was able to do this was not necessarily harmful to the true interests of those Powers
or of Europe. It can be argued, on the contrary, that
Talleyrand's participation in the conference to work
for the best possible terms for France operated as a
potent and beneficial restraint on the rapacious temp-
tations to which victors are inevitably subject.

It is further to be noted that although Castlereagh,
as Foreign Secretary, was in charge of the negotiations on the British side, he had as his principal
adviser, not another politician or even a civilian official, but a soldier. Nowadays, the Duke of Wellington would have been denied any such position. He
would have been told that his part had ended with
the cessation of active hostilities, and that the work
of peace-making would be taken over and conducted

by politicians who understood things that stupid soldiers did not.

Napoleon did his best to ruin the peace settlement for France by his escape from Elba. The Hundred Days and Waterloo played into the hands of the advocates of "toughness" among the allies, who urged a drastic revision of the former easy terms and demanded the shooting of Napoleon and stringent safeguards against further breaches of the peace by the French. It was against this outbreak of extremism that Wellington penned the above-quoted despatch to Castlereagh, in which he emphasised the unwisdom of repressive measures, whatever the provocation, as likely to cause a violent reaction by the French as soon as they felt strong enough to throw off their fetters.

It was, however, inevitable that the original proposals should be revised, though once again the moderating influence of the British and Austrian plenipotentiaries was successful in keeping the demands for punitive measures within bounds. Under the final settlement, France still received fairly generous terms. Though she was now to lose territory in Europe, it was only to re-establish her frontiers as they had been in 1789, before the French Revolution had begun; and her colonies were still to be returned to her. The chief penal clauses were an indemnity of 700 million francs and a foreign occupying force of 150,000 men. But these latter were to be confined to certain fortresses, and in the event remained in France only for three years. By 1818 they had been withdrawn and France was readmitted on equal terms to the Concert of the Great Powers of Europe. There had been no question of French disarmament.

The attitude of Castlereagh, Wellington and Metternich towards a subjugated "aggressor" and the treatment of France which was the outcome of that attitude stand in violent contrast to the treatment of Germany in virtually identical circumstances in 1919. On the latter occasion, there was harshness instead of leniency, spoliation instead of forbearance, an utter disregard of German pride, self-respect, and national feeling instead of a studied consideration for these psychological factors. Germany lost Alsace and Lorraine permanently and the Saar temporarily to France, and the more valuable parts of Upper Silesia to Poland. The German Rhineland was separated from the rest of the country and made a demilitarised area. Germany was stripped bare of colonies, which were divided between her late enemies, Britain obtaining the lion's share in spite of the declaration of her Prime Minister at the outbreak of war that she desired "no territorial aggrandisement." Colossal indemnities were demanded, which economic experts even in the victorious countries declared could not be paid. And armies of occupation, which included black troops, were quartered on Germany for periods announced to be up to 15 years. Further, these drastic enactments were arranged in conferences between the victors from which German representatives were excluded. These latter were only brought in like convicted criminals to put their signatures under duress to the conquerors' terms. How much they were under duress was shown by the fact that the terms included the deeply humiliating and entirely untrue admission that Germany alone was responsible for the war.

The notion of what constituted statesmanlike peace-making had undergone a radical change in

the 104 years since 1815. In 1919 not one of the "Big
Five" expressed any concern for German feelings or
had any thought that, as the Duke of Wellington had
believed, a good peace settlement must "suit the
interests of all parties to it," vanquished as well as
victors, and that the defeated would be more likely
to observe loyally the provisions of such a settlement
if they felt it to be reasonably fair to themselves. By
1919, the moderation and generosity of 1815 had turned
to repression, to a proclaimed determination to
"squeeze Germany till the pips squeaked."

It is a noteworthy and sorrowful example of human ingratitude that the French were foremost in
demanding the severest treatment of Germany;
that she be disarmed and kept disarmed; that she be
financially crippled by mountainous indemnities;
that the Rhineland be neutralised. There was, of
course, plenty of superficial logic on the side of these
French demands, though its superficiality should
have been readily apparent to anyone well-
grounded in the history of international statecraft,
a branch of knowledge which, however, was not a
distinguishing feature of the big figures at the Versailles Peace Conference. But, logic or no logic, the
fact remained that the drastic punishment and humiliation demanded for Germany by Clemenceau and the French was in painful contrast to the
leniency the French nation had received from its
conquerors, including the Prussians, when, in 1815,
it had stood in the same position that the German
nation did in 1919. It ill became the French of all
people to press, as they so vehemently did, for the utmost repression to be shown towards the Germans.

The vital question is not, however, one of seem-
liness but of wisdom. The peace settlements of 1815

and 1919, both following great wars, exhibit opposing doctrines. The earlier doctrine, propounded and put into practice by nineteenth-century aristocrats, was that it was dangerous for conquerors to abuse their power and that the more that a beaten nation could be made to feel it had been given a fair deal, the longer peace was likely to endure. The later doctrine, the offspring of twentieth-century democracy, was that perpetual peace could be obtained by chaining the last "aggressor" to the ground for ever.

What is the verdict of history on these rival doctrines? The moderate and generous peace settlement of 1815 was markedly successful. Except for the minor interlude of the Crimean War, France showed no actively aggressive symptoms for over half a century. From 1815 until 1870, when there was a clamour for war against Prussia, France remained quiescent. It is true that the British became fearful of a French invasion about 1859; but the scare came to nought. And even this was over 40 years after Waterloo.

On the other hand, the peace of repression of 1919 had exactly the consequences that the Duke of Wellington had predicted such a peace would have; when, as we have seen, he told Castlereagh that the crippling of France would but defer a continuance of the war until "France shall find a suitable opportunity of endeavouring to regain what she has lost." This was just what happened to Germany. Crushed and frustrated, she bided her time till, sixteen years after Versailles, she willingly brought Hitler into power in the hope that, whatever his methods, he would at least rescue the country from continuing subjection and help it regain what had been taken from it. And so he did, and by that very continuance of warlike operations which Wellington had apprehended, to the further misery and disaster of Europe. The views of the appeasing soldier of 1815 proved much more politically effica- cious than those of the "tough" journalist-politician of 1919. Yet it was this very Clemenceau who sar- castically declared that "war was much too serious a business to be left to the Generals."

The Vansittartite outcome of the 1939 war—it would be inaccurate to call it a peace settlement— outdid even Versailles in repression and chastise- ment. Not only were Germany's armed forces com- pletely disbanded but the German leaders were hanged or imprisoned. The German government was destroyed and replaced by Allied Control Com- missioners, the members of which went over, as they will tell you, with the expectation of staying for twenty years. This destruction of the central govern- ment has resulted in the division of Germany into two halves, one Communist and the other supposedly democratic; much as Britain might be divided into a Communist north of the Humber and a democratic south—or vice versa.

The division of Germany is the fruit of the Church- illian policy of extirpation as contrasted with the Wellingtonian belief in leniency and conciliation; and a very ugly fruit it is. We have no reason to suppose that the Germans will tolerate such a division of their country a moment longer than they must. Indeed, Dr. Adenauer solemnly swore on June 23rd, 1953, in front of a crowd of 500,000 people, that the western Germans would "not rest or desist until Ger- mans behind the Iron Curtain are free and united with us in freedom and peace." But we know from the wretched example of Korea that it is much easier to divide a country than to reunite it. It is fairly certain that a free vote of the whole German people would result in the eastern Germans throwing off Communism and coalescing with western Germany. It is equally certain that the East German authorities will resist a free vote to the uttermost, since it would mean their loss of power, probable exile, and possible indictment.

Should, however, the German pressure for unity become too strong to withstand, what then? Would the British and French Governments continue in their attitude of allowing Germany some armaments but only on such a limited scale as to prevent her becoming a 'menace'? If so, we should have the conditions of the 1920s and early 1930s over again, and the emergence of another Hitler would be inevitable. If the Germans should succeed in casting off the yoke of the Russians, who defeated them in the war, it is hardly to be thought that they would be content to live by permission of the French, whom they utterly defeated.

13

International Guilt and Innocence

If a third world war can be avoided, it will only be by approaching the problem with scientific objectivity. Mr. Churchill and President Roosevelt both failed to make this approach in regard to the last war and with unfortunate results. They both began with the assumption that Germany was the sole cause of the two world wars and proceeded to argue that if she could be totally defeated and disarmed, peace would reign indefinitely. But as this basic assumption was wrong, it is hardly surprising that the war policy they constructed on that false foundation collapsed in ruins as soon as the war was over.

Their attitude represented a rejection of scientific method and a return to mediaeval witch-hunting. Germany was declared to be a nation possessed by the devil, demoniacally responsible for the ills of all mankind, and it became as dangerous from 1940 to 1945 to suggest that this accusation was not in accordance with the evidence as it had been for Galileo to question in the early seventeenth century the traditional belief, officially supported by the Papacy and the Inquisition, that the sun went round the earth. Galileo's published theory to the contrary, a theory upon which all future oceanic navigation depended, was put on the Index of banned publications in 1616, and he had to repudiate what he had written under threat of torture. In like fashion, any objection to the official propaganda of the last war that the Germans were the wicked people of the world was liable to get the objector into trouble.

Yet evidence to the contrary was so extensive that anyone with even a little historical knowledge saw it staring reproachfully and accusingly through every window. The Germans may indeed be cruel monsters, given to all sorts of bestialities and atrocities. But who is not? The British put down the Indian Mutiny with a thoroughness of terror which included indiscriminate massacres of unarmed men, women and children and such supremely savage actions as the blowing of mutineers from the muzzles of guns. They preceded the Germans in the use of the concentration camp when, in the Boer War, they herded the Boer civil population into compounds under conditions which caused the deaths of no less than 10 per cent of the entire Boer people. Had this happened to the British in the last war, it would have meant the loss of five million lives.

The cruelties of the Russian Communist regime have been a political commonplace for many years. Five million peasants were deliberately starved to death in the early 1930s as an act of Government policy, and slave labour on a huge scale and under terrible conditions has been a commonplace of the Russian system since long before the last war. Fear stalks the land in Russia and its satellites as in probably no other part of the modern world. The midnight knock on the door, the removal and disappearance into oblivion of one or more members of the family, the ubiquitous spying and informing, even by supposed friends against each other and children against parents, are typical and horrible features of modern Russian life.

Early in July, 1952, a United States Congressional Committee reported that it was undoubtedly the Russians who had murdered over 4,000 Polish officers in the Katyn Forest in 1940, and another 10,000 elsewhere.* "There can be no doubt," said the Committee, "that this massacre was a calculated plot to eliminate all Polish leaders who subsequently would have opposed the Soviet's plans for communising Poland." At the Nuremberg trials, the Russian prosecutor accused the Germans of the Katyn murders. But the Tribunal evidently had its misgivings about this accusation, for the matter was not proceeded with, although no attempt was made to discover who, in fact, had done the murdering. If the American Congressional Committee's conclusion is a sound one, it follows that the Russian judge on the Nuremberg tribunal was representative of a country guilty of as pretty a war crime as anything that was brought against the Germans.

The Chinese, of course, have been famous for cruelty brought to a fine art for a very long time. Torture has been so much taken for granted in that country that cheap toys showing its more common forms were among the ordinary stock-in-trade of knick-knack shops when the author first went to the China Station in 1913. Since the advent of the Communist government, purges and liquidations have proceeded in the best Russian fashion, a particularly

* London "Daily Telegraph" of 3rd July, 1952.

gruesome account of the public trials of those marked down for elimination appearing in *"The Listener"* of May 15, 1952.

It was stated that these trials take place before large audiences of 20,000 or more, the prisoners being tried in batches with their hands bound behind their backs. Placed among the audience are agents to lead the cheering of the prosecution or shout abuse of the prisoners as required. After their own statements of the prisoners' offences, the official prosecutors then ask for members of the audiences to testify against the accused. The same agents go up, work themselves up into a fury of denunciation, spit on the prisoners, kick them, and tug out their beards. The audience is then asked what should be done, and the pre-organised reply thunders back, "Away with them, kill them"; anyone not conforming being in danger of joining the next batch of prisoners himself. The condemned men are then executed in front of the crowd, in response to the "unanimous demand of the people."

There is no need to enlarge upon the cruelties practised by the Japanese. They were kept well before the British public's notice during the last war. Just across the way are the South Koreans, for whose benefit the U.N. war in Korea has been fought. This is what a British War Correspondent wrote about them. 'Round Seoul the execution squads of Syngman Rhee had begun to work so feverishly and ferociously at their murderous tasks that a great wave of indignation swept through all those who saw and heard. Men and women (and even children, it was reliably written) were dragged from the prisons of Seoul, marched to fields on the outskirts of the town, and shot carelessly and callously in droves and shovelled into trenches'.*

* *Cry Korea*—R. Thompson, p. 273 (Macdonald).

Atrocities committed by the Turks against the Armenians, Bulgars, and other of their subject races were intermittent causes of political agitations in Britain during the nineteenth century, demands for punitive action against these "butchers" being made by public men contemporaneously with the uncondemned blowing of rebels from British guns in India.

France, often held up nowadays as a model of civilisation in contradistinction to brutal and barbaric Germany, was the originator of terror methods in the Revolution of 1789. That, of course, everybody knows. What is hardly known at all in Britain is that an even greater terror took place in 1944-46, when there was an orgy of summary executions of alleged Pétainists and collaborationists by Communists, "resistance" men, and returned Gaullists, the latter anxious to show their *émigré* patriotism by the slaughter and persecution of their fellow-countrymen who had stayed to face the music of enemy occupation. The French Government has officially admitted to over 10,000 executions of this kind, but private estimates put the total at more like 100,000. This is how Sisley Huddleston describes the sort of thing that went on:

"Many of those they (the *Épurateurs*) called for questioning did not survive the ordeal. In the hotels which served as prisons, women of the streets were called in to gloat over victims (among them high officials) who were compelled to turn round in circles and to cry "Maréchal, nous voilà!" as they were beaten with bludgeons or cowhide whips. Some of the victims were branded, or burnt with cigarettes (the breasts of women were thus disfigured). . . . There were fiendishly ingenious applications of electrical apparatus, both external and internal."*

* *"Pétain, Patriot, or Traitor?"* Sisley Huddleston, p. 247.

The crude Teuton, Himmler, and his acolytes had, it would seem, something to learn from the more refined and artistic Latins to the westward.

On January 23, 1949, the *Sunday Pictorial* published, under the headline "AMERICANS TORTURE GERMANS TO EXTORT 'CONFESSIONS,' " what it called "an ugly story of barbarous tortures inflicted in the name of allied justice," taken from the report of the American Judge Edward L. van Roden, who had investigated allegations to this effect as a member of an official Commission of Enquiry. The Judge found that German prisoners were subjected to various forms of maltreatment till, as the *Pictorial* said, "strong men were reduced to broken wrecks ready to mumble any admission demanded by their prosecutors."

Some of the actual methods of persuasion revealed by the Judge included forcing lighted matches under prisoners' fingernails, kicking in the testicles beyond repair (in all but 2 of the 139 cases investigated), putting a black hood over a prisoner's head and then bashing him in the face with knuckle-dusters, and the use of bogus priests, complete with crucifix and candles, to hear confessions in the hope of gaining incriminating information.

How can it be maintained, in view of all the foregoing, that the Germans are unique monsters of cruelty and sadism, as so many good people in Britain are convinced they are and declare them to be? Monsters they may be, but unique, no. When we go to church and recite with the vicar our confession as "miserable sinners," we recognise that we may have a few blemishes ourselves. But in relation to a foreign enemy, we leave this penitent mood behind us as we pass the church door. Once back in the cheerful

sunlight, we replace our tribal headgear and, led by
the vicar banging the tom-tom, we work up another
high pressure of indignation against the enemy's wickedness. It is they and not we ourselves who are the
sinners.

A few years ago, I happened to be in Germany and
was discussing the war with a German ex-naval officer. "But you see," I said in the course of discussion,
"we were told we were fighting for Christian civilisation and human decency." To my astonishment, an
astonishment I now realise to have been pathetically
naïve, he replied, "and so were we."

Hypocrisy is never a lovable characteristic and
can be harmful as well as unlikable, and to suffer
disadvantage and even to risk acute danger for its indulgence is comparable to drinking to the point of
delirium tremens. But that is precisely the position
in which very large numbers of the British have been
placed by the hatred propaganda of the war years.
Any suggestion that we might make friends with the
Germans is as likely as not to be met with the reply,
"the Germans? Oh! no, we couldn't make friends with
them after all they've done!" Well, maybe; but in that
case, whom can we make friends with, after all
they've done, too? If one approaches the matter from
the point of view of a genuine seeker after objective
data, there do not seem to be any foreign hands we
can soil our own immaculate ones by shaking. That is
always supposing ours are immaculate; and that, I
fear, is at least open to question if we can bring ourselves to examine all the evidence about ourselves,
and not only the part we want to examine.

Take, for instance, the accusation so often levelled
against the Germans, as a reason for their moral os-
tracism, of having starved 20,000 people to death in

Belsen and other camps. On the 13th and 14th of February, 1945, Dresden was attacked by British and American bombers at a time when it was crowded with refugees, mostly women and children, fleeing from the advancing Russian armies. The slaughter and maiming were appalling. About 25,-000 people were killed and 30,000 injured in a night and day of horror when crowds of the homeless and helpless refugees "surged this way and that for hours in search of a place of safety in a strange city amid bursting bombs, burning phosphorus and falling buildings."* Did the British press express any concern over this holocaust among German civilians, including a high proportion of women and children? Not at all; the bulk of it printed gleeful comments that the extra death-roll represented "an unexpected and fortunate bonus" to the bombers' activities. Do episodes like this—Dresden was not the only one of its kind by any means—leave the British (or Americans) entitled to point the finger of scorn at Belsen or Buchenwald or indeed any other place where the Germans can be said to have acted with brutality?

Indeed, the frequent attitude displayed by members of the British public that the German hand is the only one (except possibly the Japanese) that is too dirty to be taken ignores the turn that has been given to propaganda by post-war events. Even if such people have heard nothing about the French *épuration* and have next to no knowledge of what is happening in China or of the shadier parts of Turkish, American, and British history, they ought to know that if there is anything to choose between the habits of the

---

* *Advance to Barbarism*—F. J. P. Veale (Merrymeade Publishing Co. and C. C. Nelson Co., Appleton, Wis.), p. 125. There are other estimators who, however, put the loss of life much higher, even at 250,000.

Russians and the Germans it is now officially in favour of the Germans, since it has hardly been possible to pick up a paper during the last five years without reading the opinions of prominent politicians, archbishops, and others that the Russian aggressions, tyrannies, slave labour camps, political trials, and torture of prisoners are "the worst in history"; which must mean that they are worse than anything the Germans did in that line.* Yet there are plenty of men and women in all walks of life who are only too anxious to "come to an understanding with Russia" and would be prepared for considerable sacrifices to that end if only the Russians would "show a little sense and friendliness." Then why not with Germany?

Why not with Germany? Because the brains of the bulk of the British are still semi-anaesthetised by the propaganda of the war years. "If a thing is said often enough it becomes true" is a well known journalistic dictum: and the villainy of the Germans was stressed so continuously between 1939 and 1946 or 1947 that most of the British acquired a mental fixation to that effect and so find it extremely difficult to readjust their minds to a different outlook. They find it difficult because of a natural disinclination to revise an opinion they have long and passionately held; because they have an unpleasant feeling that there is a risk of unpopularity in saying anything favourable about the ex-enemy who was lately so much reviled, and because they have an instinctive fear of something worse. The memory lingers that not so very long ago it was actually dangerous to do anything but blackguard the Germans. From 1940 till 1945, anyone expressing any sympathy

---

* In June 1952 ("Daily Telegraph" of 30.6.52), the United States Government turned over to the United Nations a dossier of evidence about Russian forced labour, said to constitute "the worst slavery in history."

for the German enemy was liable to find himself in prison and treated as a common criminal. And so, in spite of the post-war emergence of a new menace altogether, in spite of the official encouragement of the Germans to rearm, and not only encouragement to rearm but threats that they must, the bulk of the British still persist in regarding the Germans as a world menace and an outcast nation with which no decent people will associate. The British who take that line are undoubtedly blind to the certainty that they are thereby assisting the cause of hostile Russian Communism. Never have boomerangs returned so accurately to smite the throwers as the British hatred campaign against the Germans, and Regulation 18B.

14

Advantages of
Negotiated Peace

The last chapter will, I hope, have convinced the reader that the national approach to international affairs can be the reverse of scientific. For there are, of course, no such things as wicked nations and virtuous nations, and any suggestion to the contrary is nonsense. All nations are mixtures of wickedness and virtue, as they always have been and will ever remain. And if one nation manifests some unpleasant characteristic in a specially vicious form, the odds are that balancing nastinesses can be found in the others from which the first is relatively free. Those who talk most loudly about the brotherhood of man will not allow themselves to recognise its brotherhood in villainy.

There is need to stress the marked differences that exist between individuals and groups in the matter of general morality. The individual is in a much weaker position than malefactors in the mass. If convicted, he commonly loses the sympathy of his fellows, and should he be executed for his offence, he is silenced for ever.

This does not happen in the case of collective misdemeanours. If the group be large enough, powerful enough, and permanent enough, its members fortify each other in defying, even if they cannot deny, accusations of moral infirmity. They defy such accusations on the simple and generally quite truthful argument that whatever they themselves may have done their accusers are no better. We find this rule in operation wherever groups are in conflict. It is a commonplace that political parties resort to questionable conduct which their individual members would scorn to practise in their private lives. If, as the saying is, diplomats are honourable men who lie abroad for the good of their country, it could also be said that politicians are honourable men who lie at home for the good of their party. Any such lapses from veracity do not affect the consciences of the vicarious prevaricators. The burden of guilt varies inversely with the number of persons sharing it, until it ceases to be felt at all.

It is therefore supremely stupid to complain that the Germans are "manufacturing excuses for their own defeat" or "trying to put the blame for the war on someone else." That is the way all powerful groups behave, and will always behave, and usually they have some degree of justification for so doing. You never hear a political party publicly ascribing its defeat to its own shortcomings in office. It is always due to the dishonest machinations of the other side. Nor can I recall a single case of a trade union admitting it was in the wrong in calling a strike. If the strike is unsuccessful, the usual excuse is that the long-suffering workmen were overborne by the superior resources of the employers, and we are told that the men went back to work with a sullen feeling of resentment and a determination to get their own back next time.

No intelligent person ought therefore to be surprised at Germans or Japanese or any other nation reacting to defeat in a similar fashion, especially as a high degree of cunning is seldom needed in devising a suitable *tu quoque* to incriminatory victors. For instance, a German would have to be very dull-witted if, in contemplating the many British indictments of Teutonic "aggression," he did not call to mind that the far-flung aggregation of territory once known as the British Empire hardly came into being as a result of spontaneous bursts of affection by Red Indians, Cypriots, Boers, Bantus, Indians, Burmese, Malayans, Australian Black fellows, and Maoris. And if the general run of the British have no knowledge of the fact that the French under Louis XIV ravaged Germany from one end to the other and that the French Emperor Napoleon I made himself exceedingly unpleasant to the Germans of a hundred and forty-odd years ago, the latter have by no means forgotten these historical episodes. Moreover, a German might reasonably regard it as peculiar that a nation, to whom the international sobriquet of *perfidious Albion* has notoriously been applied, should set itself up as an instructor of the German people in moral rectitude while at the same time laying claim to a strong sense of humour.

History supports the view that there is little to choose between the moral worth of one nation and another; and that, failing exceptional influences, they will all behave in roughly similar fashion in similar circumstances. We declared before the war that absolute power had corrupted Hitler. But when the

unconditional surrender of Germany had given us
and our allies absolute power in the Germany we
were occupying, we then became corrupted ourselves. At the very selfsame time that we were bringing charges of looting conquered countries against
the German leaders on trial at Nuremberg, we were
all busy looting Germany on a huge scale. Not only
were personal possessions being filched by the occupying forces, service and civilian, but an organised
campaign of plunder of factories and machinery of
vast dimensions was under way on the plea of repara-
tions. Even private yachts from Kiel and other harbours were seized and sailed or transported to England.
In the occupation of Paris in 1915, the Duke of Wellington enforced an exactly opposite code of conduct.*

This was not the only way, as we have noted in
previous chapters, in which the British approach to
warfare in Wellington's time differed from that of the
present day. The two attitudes, of then and now,
present indeed a marked, almost a fundamental,
contrast. The earlier period is distinguished by a
limited war effort, a husbanding of the national resources, the utmost political indulgence towards the
enemy, and a scrupulous respect for his private
property: the later by an unlimited war aim pushed
to the farthest extreme, reckless expenditure, a complete disregard of enemy susceptibilities, and a ruthless destruction of civilian property during the war and
confiscation of it afterwards. War and warlike processes as understood by the Duke of Wellington were
obviously of a different nature from the same things
as seen by Mr. Churchill.

---

* There is a story that the Duke personally unhooked pictures in the
Louvre for transfer to England. If so, he took care that no one else
should behave thus.

Even the attitude to peace of the early nineteenth century had undergone a striking change by the twentieth. In 1801, after eight years of warfare against revolutionary France and at a time when not only was the defeat of the enemy not in prospect but the balance of overall warlike advantage was very much on his side, Britain was ready to make peace and did make it, with considerable concessions to the French enemy. The war broke out again two years later. But three years after that, early in 1806, Britain was putting out peace feelers; although Napoleon, so far from being on the down grade, was on the threshold of the most brilliantly successful part of his military career. The British leaders of those days evidently had no objection to patched-up compromise peaces which left the enemy in a favourable position.

By the twentieth century, something had happened to alter this outlook. In the 1914-18 war, peace unaccompanied by victory had become suspect. In 1917, when the terrible deadlock on the western front had persisted for two years with fearful bloodshed and no sign of a break-through by either side, Lord Lansdowne decided that the only sane solution to such apparently meaningless carnage was to conclude a peace. But when his project became known, he was regarded almost as a hostile conspirator, and the *Times* refused to publish the letter in which he set out his peace plan.

By 1939 the word peace had become almost synonymous with treason. Even before the war had begun, the British press was referring to "peace threats," and the several wartime peace offers made to Britain by Germany were mentioned by the Government, if they were mentioned at all, with a scorn and derision in which all patriotic citizens were clearly expected to join. Hitler made two such offers, one in October, 1939, after the defeat of Poland, and the next in July, 1940, after the defeat of France. It is conceivable that these were sinister plots on Hitler's part to lure Britian to her undoing. Yet they were logical enough from his point of view. His initial object had been to crush Poland and recover the Polish Corridor. This achieved, he proposed to the guarantors of Poland, who had been unable to fulfil their guarantee, that hostilities should cease. When they refused, his object became that of breaking the Anglo-French combination against Germany. This Hitler also achieved, and once more he suggested to the surviving enemy that there was not much point in going on with the war.

There was, too, the peace offer of 1942, already mentioned, made by German anti-Hitler plotters through the Bishop of Chichester. But this, as we have seen, was brushed aside by the British Cabinet.

These successive British refusals even to examine enemy proposals for peace coincided with a strident propaganda that the British were the peace-lovers and the Germans the war-mongers of the time. We British often accuse the Russians of having introduced into the world the particularly vile device of disseminating mental confusion by using words in the opposite sense of what they have hitherto been understood to convey. But this misuse of the word "peace-loving" by ourselves seems to indicate that the disease has been more widespread than we have thought. For although the British Government may (or may not) have had good and adequate reasons for rejecting all German peace offers out of hand, such rejections were hardly certificates of a passionate love of peace.

For Britain to have made peace with Germany in 1939 (if France had agreed) would have meant acquiescing in the German defeat of Poland, admitting the failure of the British guarantee, and therefore eating decidedly humble pie. To have made peace in 1940, after the fall of France, would have been even more humiliating. Yet, before such a possibility be dismissed by the reader as unthinkable, it is at least worth remembering that our predecessors of the year after Trafalgar, whom we are not in the habit of regarding as poltroons, were ready to consider peace with Napoleon almost immediately after he had decisively beaten the Austrians at Austerlitz. And not merely to consider peace. They directed Lord Yarmouth in Paris to propose it.*

It may well be that peace with Germany either in 1939 or 1940 was out of the question. The same cannot, however, be said about the underground peace offer of 1942, for by that time Britain's earlier reverses had been retrieved and it was obvious that Germany could not defeat her enemies. Britain could therefore have made peace with full dignity. But then, of course, if your national object is not political but military, if what you are seeking is the complete overthrow of the enemy, then any suggestion of peace is indeed a threat.

There is nothing in history to suggest that any reasonable offer of peace, made at a reasonably sensible time, should not be sincerely examined and

---

* Lord Yarmouth had been interned in France, but was used as the British Government's agent, being released by the French for this purpose.

if possible accepted. The enemy may have hidden designs for using peace to gain some advantage for himself and thus to lead you into a trap. But there is no absolute reason why he should be successful if you take proper precautions, while he is inevitably taking some risk, if his real intentions remain aggressive, in making peace at all. For it is always easier to keep an existing war going than to restart one after a pause. The Peace Party of a country, whether that country be democratic or authoritarian—and every country has a Peace Party—is bound to become more influential in peace than in war; while the ordinary civil population, having enjoyed some relief from war and its dangers and restrictions and been buoyed up with greater hope for the survival of sons and husbands, is likely to show greater resistance to the revival of a war that has once been checked than to the continuance of one that has never been stopped. Maybe a peace so concluded will not last, as in the case of the Peace of Amiens. But its short duration is no evidence that that Peace was a mistake. It was probably better than no peace at all.

It is noteworthy that it is almost invariably this principle of "peace whenever possible," and not "a fight to a finish" which governs the official advice to civil disputants in Britain. It is to settlements out of court that judges give their principal blessing, with voluntary settlements during the hearing of the case as the next best thing. Litigants making such arrangements, instead of pressing matters to the end, are nearly always told by the bench that they have acted wisely. In industrial disputes, the government does all it can to promote "conciliation" and to get the "fight" ended as quickly as possible by a settlement acceptable to both sides. Ministers who apply the machinery of mediation in cases of industrial trouble are therefore in tune with the Ministers who concluded the Peace of Amiens in 1801 and who told Lord Yarmouth in Paris to seek an arrangement with Napoleon in 1806, but not with the Churchillian policy of no compromise, unconditional surrender, and an automatic refusal of all peace offers.

The great defect of the latter policy, and especially of its concentration on complete victory, is that if successful it conduces inevitably to abuse of power, which in turn is an enemy of peace. On the whole, humanity is not bellicose, the bulk of the people being ordinarily governed by the instinct of live and let live, and as long as most men feel they are getting a reasonably square deal they have little inclination to go on the warpath. But let them acquire a sense of injustice and they become ready material for the trouble-maker. Nor is there a surer way of giving them this feeling of injustice than abuse of power of which they are the victims. Human nature being what it is, wisdom in the use of power is more likely in proportion as unwisdom would be difficult or dangerous; and the more complete a victory, the greater the temptation to give rein to vengeance, arrogance, and greed. But the more such temptation is surrendered to, the more numerous are the dragons' teeth that are thereby sown.

Of this, there are plenty of illustrations in the history of the last 150 years. We have already noticed how beneficial was the forbearance and moderation shown to the vanquished French in 1815. Another example of the same sort is provided by the action of the British in giving the defeated Boers an equal share in the government of a unified South Africa.

In spite of their ingrained dislike, even hatred, of the British, and in spite of the recent decimation of their women and children and old people in the British concentration camps, this generous treatment of the Boers has served to keep South Africa within the Commonwealth partnership since the end of the Boer War, and to bring South African armies of Boers and Britons to fight on the British side in two wars against Germany. And when, in the first of those wars, a Boer revolt did break out, it was put down by a force under the command of a Boer General. It was then that General Smuts declared: "I stand for England; a country which, when it had us at its mercy, treated us as a Christian nation should." There could be no more eloquent testimony to the psychological effect of international generosity to the defeated.

It is hardly to be doubted that had a Versailles Treaty been imposed on the Boers such as was done to the Germans in 1919, they would have seized upon England's extremity of 1914 as the Boer opportunity for a national uprising, as the southern Irish did (unsuccessfully) in 1916. As it is, though the South African ties with the Commonwealth have suffered and are still suffering stress and strain, the connection has held for 50 years. South Africa could have seceded at will any time since the Statute of Westminster, and if she has not, it is undoubtedly because she has had insufficient grievance to form a strong enough rallying cry for secession.

It is clear from their writings that Lord Vansittart and others like him do not think the victorious allies abused their power in the case of the Treaty of Versailles; but—what is more important—the Germans did think so. The war had arisen over the question of whether the Serbs should be allowed to murder Austria's Crown Prince with impunity, and ended with the complete collapse of Germany and absolute power for the victors to decide her fate in any way they pleased, provided they were prepared to dishonour the conditions they had offered her as a basis for surrender: and they were so prepared. By their dictated peace, Germany lost all her colonies all over the world, the Saar to France for fifteen years, the richest part of Silesia and the Danzig Corridor to Poland, and her only remaining ally in forcible disintegration. It was much as if the collapse of the British General Strike in 1926 had been followed by the abolition of the Trades Union Congress, the confiscation of all its funds, life sentences for its principal officials, and the demolition of Transport House. But the Prime Minister's (Mr. Baldwin's) attitude towards the strike was; no recriminations, no apportionment of blame, let byegones be byegones and look forward and not back. If those principles were appropriate to an internal dispute, why not also to an external one?

Unlike the Boers, who were ready to accept the Act of Union as a reasonably just solution of the South African problem, the Germans were left by the Treaty of Versailles with a bitter sense of grievance which eventually made them welcome Hitler and his Nazis as deliverers from bondage. Six years later, or 21 years after the armistice of 1918, Germany was again at war. Even if Dr. Malan were to declare South Africa a republic tomorrow, generosity in the case of the Boers will have paid over twice as long a dividend as repression in the case of the Germans.

As for the treatment of the Germans in 1945, I do not think that even Lord Vansittart would pretend that they would be likely to regard it as a model of gentlemanly moderation, precluding any need to work for the cancellation of the conditions they were forced to accept.

It is often alleged that, had the Germans been victorious in either Great War, they would have done far worse things to us than we did to them. But this is naturally an unverifiable supposition, since they were not victorious. It is true that a German document was discovered after the collapse of 1945, said to be a plan to pastoralise England and make a drastic reduction in her population. This document, assuming it to be authentic, provides no proof that the plan it contained would have been carried out. Curiously enough, another plan was in preparation in the United States at about the same time for dealing with Germany in almost identical fashion. The author is conceded to have been one Harry Dexter White, who persuaded a willing Henry Morgenthau to sponsor it. But the Morgenthau plan, though approved by President Roosevelt, was not, when it came to the point, put into practise. And, naturally, its German counterpart might have suffered the same fate. The existence of a plan, however ferocious, is no guarantee of its execution.

The only concrete evidence we have since 1815 of German treatment of a fallen foe after peace had returned* is to be found in Bismarck's three wars of 1864, 1866, and 1870. In these, the German behaviour to the defeated enemy was outstandingly tolerant. Indeed, in the wars against Denmark and Austria, the prizes Bismarck collected were confined, with disciplined restraint, to those objectives for which he had gone to war. He wanted the Duchies

---

* The treatment of Russia in 1917 and of France, Poland, and Jugoslavia in 1939-41 was while hostilities were still in progress.

of Schleswig and Holstein, and he took them. Otherwise, he left the Danes unharmed and unplundered. From Austria, Bismarck wanted nothing but a recognition of German hegemony in the German world, and he demanded nothing more.

In the case of France, Bismarck went slightly further. His main object in fighting the French was not to plunder them but to unify Germany. Nevertheless, plunder them he did—by annexing Alsace and Lorraine and by levying a war indemnity. Both these predatory actions, which were a surrender to greed and therefore amounted to abuse of power, were to have most unfortunate consequences for their perpetrators. For the acquisition of Alsace and Lorraine was a primary cause of the ensuing French bitterness towards Germany which led to a French resolve to get the provinces back, if necessary by war. As for the war indemnity, it formed an immediate precedent which was to recoil with devastating effect on Germany's own head when she herself was beaten in 1918. And not much imagination is needed to picture what we British have invited for ourselves by what we demanded from Germany in that way at Versailles, and what we stripped from her after 1945, should we ever be so unfortunate as to be unsuccessful in war ourselves.

To do justice to Bismarck, however, it should be recorded that it was with reluctance that he agreed to the acquisition of Alsace and Lorraine. These he did not want to take from France, but demanded them on the insistence of the German generals, who said they were necessary for strategic defence. The moral is to the physical, said Napoleon, as three is to one; and the ill-feeling caused by the German seizure of these strategical bastions led in the long run not to strategical security but to strategical disaster. Bismarck may have been conscious of this danger. At all events, he was against the acquisition of the provinces, though to be sure the Germans had quite a respectable claim to them as ancient German territory; just as good a one, in fact, as the Spanish claim to Gibraltar, which has never been surrendered.

As for the indemnity, there was, of course, nothing novel about it. The allies had taken an indemnity from France in 1815, and Napoleon had done the same to Prussia just before. Taken all round, Bismarck affords as notable an example of the wise use of power as is to be found. But then Bismarck was not, as Lord Vansittart says, a crafty Prussian bully but was, with Castlereagh, Metternich and Wellington, one of the great statesmen of European history.

15

The Prospect of Europe

And so we come to the final stage of this investigation.
For I propose now to examine what can best be done
to meet the critical situation in which Europe finds
itself, in the light of the evidence surveyed in the foregoing chapters. In setting about this task, I shall follow the formula recommended to be used as a standard by the service staff colleges for thinking out
problems of this nature and which has, in fact, been
so used in practice for several generations. This se-
quence of thought runs according to the following
headings:

1. Review of the situation.
2. What is our object?
3. What are our possible courses of action for achieving
   our object (with an assessment of their relative
   merits)?
4. Our proposed course of action.

The review of the situation has, of course, been
conducted in the previous part of this book. The

fairly lengthy consideration devoted thereto will, I hope, have clarified the subject for the general reader by exposing a number of serious misconceptions widely held regarding it, and by clearing away most of the intellectual drift wood that has piled up round it to such a height as largely to obscure the essential matter in the middle. Perhaps the chief points worth repeating here are that Germany is not the master aggressor of history that she has so often been declared to be since 1939, that the Germans are no worse than other peoples of the world, and that the British have often allied themselves to Germany (or a part thereof) in the past and need not hesitate to do so again, should it suit their purpose.

I will now pass on to the object. My choice for this is a modification of that declared by the Duke of Wellington to be Britain's "great object" in his letter to Castlereagh quoted in Chapter 12; namely: "peace for a few years." My own version is "peace for as long as possible." It is not peace for evermore, since that is unattainable. War cannot be abolished in this world. Two wars to end war have, as we have previously noticed, been utter failures in that respect; and have indeed resulted in making wars rather more frequent than before and the world in general rather more quarrelsome.

There has been much loose talk since 1918 of the rule of law as a substitute for force. But as law itself is dependent on force for its effectiveness, the antithesis is a false one. Without the police behind the law and the soldiery behind the police, law would be no more than an exercise in theoretical abstractions. Nor does law by any means concern itself only with questions of justice and equity. It has become to some extent the instrument for executing the will of the strongest, of the electoral majority, of the big battalions, who are in a position to take what they want from the minority solely because they can get it. The policy of "soaking the rich" by penal taxation and crippling death duties, imposed by virtue of majority voting power, is identical in principle to a foreign state, by virtue of its superior military strength, seizing territory belonging to another but weaker nation. The only discernible difference is in nomenclature. For whereas the latter process is described as "aggression" and is now officially listed as a crime, the former is known (in Britain) as "social justice" and is popularly regarded as self-evidently moral, progressive, and enlightened.

Politicians who pay verbal homage to the early abolition of war are preaching the impossible; and by so behaving are encouraging the peoples they address to harbour a lot of false ideals and conceptions which can do them no good. If the ordinary man can be led to think that war is on the point of being outlawed, he will naturally take no interest in how best to conduct what is obsolescent. He will therefore be predisposed, should war come after all, to accept and promote a degree of savagery in its execution which he would otherwise reject. For if he thinks that the war in progress may possibly be the last, provided the then enemy can be utterly overthrown, he is unlikely to boggle at extreme measures being taken to secure the overthrow. Yet if war be, in fact, a permanent feature of international life, a general ignorance on the part of the public about its main aspects is a national misfortune, leaving the population almost helpless to discriminate between good strategy and bad, sound leadership and unsound.

But though perpetual peace is unattainable, it does not seem impossible, if matters are properly arranged, to have peace for quite a time. Japan, for instance, enjoyed a freedom from external war for two and a half centuries, mainly by following an isolationist policy and minding her own business. Let me therefore repeat my object, which is the crux of the whole problem. It is: *Peace for as long as possible.*

Now let us proceed to consider the possible ways of achieving this object. There are already two propositions in the field for the maintenance of peace, and I will take these first. They are: (a) world government and (b) the establishment of a North Atlantic Treaty Organisation of "free" Western nations in opposition to a Communist East.

The idea of a single world government controlling the whole planet has many supporters. There are, however, several important objections to be made to it. The first is that it has always failed under test. The Holy Alliance of 1815 proved quite ineffective. The League of Nations of 1919-39 was a lamentable failure as a preserver of peace. When given a trial under almost ideal conditions in the case of the anti-Italian sanctions over Abyssinia, it proved utterly useless; and it was equally helpless to prevent in 1939 the outbreak of the most destructive war in history, a war which the League's previous futility had in fact done much to bring about by driving Italy into the arms of Germany.

The League's successor, the United Nations, provided with what was claimed to be a magical set of international dentures, broke apart almost as soon as it was formed; and what was left of it has not been a guardian of the peace but a bellows for blowing a small conflagration into a major blaze. Strategically, it would not have mattered a row of pins if the North Koreans had overrun the whole of South Korea. As the Americans possessed and still possess unchallengeable command of the sea, the North Koreans could have got no further. But the weakness (and danger) of an international peace organisation "with teeth" is that it must always fight. A sovereign state can stand knocks to its prestige without overmuch damage. An armed U.N. must take up every challenge or collapse.

It can be and has been argued that the League would have succeeded *if only* the United States had supported it, and the United Nations *if only* the Russians had not behaved so awkwardly after 1945. The decisive fact remains that they did so conduct themselves; and, moreover, these two if-onlys are not the only ifs in the case. However, the point that really matters is that both the League of Nations and the United Nations have failed as war-preventers.

The second objection to a world government plan is that many of the statements made in connection therewith seem to be palpably in conflict with the evidence. Thus, Mr. Sebastian Haffner, in a lecture to the members of the Royal United Service Institution on 31 October, 1951, expressed the opinion that:

". . . one overwhelming aspect of world affairs begins to impress itself upon us, and that is the enormous pull towards world unity. This may sound a little surprising in view of the many wars, conflicts, and crises with which we have been plagued these last 30 or 40 years, but I suggest to you that these very wars, upheavals and conflicts are part of this enormous historic development towards a unified world civilisation and a united political world organisation."

To me, it certainly is surprising to be told that frequently recurring wars, antagonisms and crises are evidence of increasing world unity. In fact, I can see nothing but fallacy in such an argument. If the world were really drawing closer together, one would expect to find established groupings, such as the British and Dutch Empires, remaining intact but coalescing into larger groupings still. But instead it seems perfectly plain that the trend is centrifugal rather than centripetal. Increased fragmentation is the dominant political phenomenon of the world since 1918. The Austrian Empire was broken up in 1919 to make the three separate States of Austria, Hungary, and Czechoslovakia, and to convert Serbia into Jugoslavia. Poland was resurrected at the expense of Russia, Germany, and Austria. Finland was created at the expense of Russia, as were Latvia, Lithuania, and Esthonia, though the last three have since disappeared; not, however, through a trend towards world unity but through vulgar conquest by the Russians. Further, the Turkish Empire was dissolved to give place to no less than six new countries; namely, Iraq, Lebanon, Syria, Palestine, Trans-Jordan, Saudi Arabia, and Egypt.

Since 1945, the Dutch Empire has been destroyed in order to create the new State of Indonesia. The great Anglo-Indian Empire has also fallen to pieces to make the three States of Pakistan, India, and Burma. Southern Ireland has seceded from the British Commonwealth and become a separate Republic, and Iceland has cut adrift from Denmark. And all over the world, in India, China, Australia, South Africa, the Argentine and elsewhere there is a pronounced movement for economic self-sufficiency and independence of foreign trade. How anyone can see in all this an "enormous historic development towards a unified world civilisation and a united political world organisation" is beyond me.

But the capacity of the British "internationalists" for self-deception is well established. The Socialists of this persuasion allowed themselves to think for many years that the world was made up of tyrannical employers and groaning masses of workers, the latter only awaiting the advent of Socialism to smite off their chains and fall sobbing with joy on each others' necks. And since Russia was already Socialist, it followed that a socialist government in Britain would enable "left to speak to left" and thus for all points of friction between the two peoples to be easily and quickly resolved.

The pain and grief in Socialist circles in Britain could hardly have been greater when it was discovered after 1945 that the so-called Left in Russia had no desire whatever to link arms with Mr. Attlee's Government; that, indeed, it regarded the British Left with rather more dislike and distrust than the British Right. The root of this disconcerting paradox lay in the fact that the British Socialists had for long been scrutinising the world through distorting lenses. They did not regard foreign peoples as Russians, Chinese, Hindus, Frenchmen, or Persians, each with their own different mentality and outlook, but as Russian-, Chinese-, Hindustani-, French-, or Persian-speaking Englishmen.

Nor is a world government to be regarded as necessarily desirable in itself. A world organisation would put immense power into the hands of the members of the world government: immense, almost unchallengeable, power if, as many of the "one-worlders" advocate, all national armed forces were abolished and military power reserved for the use of the world controllers. These, it is said, would maintain peace and order by means of an international bomber force, which would presumably be sent to punish Britain or any other country needing what the controllers regarded as a stimulus to good discipline and proper subordination to the supreme government of the world.

There is no reason to suppose that the world governors would be models of virtuous benevolence. As the whole of the non-Nazi world agreed, absolute power had a disastrously corrupting effect on Adolf Hitler, even when there were a number of outside, well-armed, and most unfriendly powers whose opinions it was unsafe for him to ignore. And if so, there is an obvious possibility that a world government which controlled all the armed force in the world could lead to the most completely corrupt and towering tyranny of which the world has yet had experience.

There are important safeguards in plurality of sovereignties; not the least of which is the provision of at least some sanctuary of escape from oppression. In Britain, we have had a taste of over-centralisation of power since 1945, and even many Socialists were dismayed to find that it led towards the same consequences of corruption and despotism as it had in Germany.

The one-worlders also seem to overlook the story of the Tower of Babel which, since it must be classed as Holy Writ, can be regarded as Divine disapproval of the World Government conception.

Nothing could have exceeded the fanfare of propaganda with which the United Nations Organisation came into being. Yet the flags were hardly hoisted and the first tax-free pay checks made out before the Rus-

sians brutally confounded the one-world plan by splitting the organisation into two opposing parts.

The North Atlantic Treaty Organisation is a recognition of this division and an impromptu attempt
to consolidate the non-Communist nations as a militarily integrated unity. As a makeshift arrangement it may be useful, but as a permanent or semi-
permanent policy it should be viewed with caution,
especially as it is unlikely to promote our object
of peace for as long as possible. For the division
of the world into two huge power blocs is to place
it in a highly brittle and insecure condition. Two,
and only two, rivals who have no other outlet for
their mutual antipathy than to snarl at and arm
against each other, and who have no other influence
to exercise restraint on either of them, are in continuous danger of coming to blows as the natural relief to overstrained nerves. For the preservation of
peace, at least a third bloc (and preferably more) is
urgently required as an alternative repository of
power which, if it were strong enough to sway the
balance between the other two blocs, could operate
to prevent their animosities from degenerating into
violence; and which would also, by its mere existence, diminish those animosities by attracting some
of the suspicion and dislike to itself.

From the European point of view, moreover, the
North Atlantic Treaty Organisation must be regarded as unstable, because it has its roots in the
United States. The Americans openly regard N.A.T.O.
as a means of defending America in Europe, of letting
Western Germany, France, and Britain bear the brunt
of an East-West war and thus keep American soil inviolate in any clash between American and Russian
ambitions and fears. For this purpose, the Americans

are prepared to provide arms and money to keep friendly European forces in the field against militant Communism—an arrangement about which we British at all events cannot complain, since we followed just the same policy in Napoleon's time and before.

Up to now, the Americans have also maintained troops in Europe, and the White House periodically issues assurances that this policy will be continued. Such assurances would, however, inspire greater confidence were not the one real guarantee lacking of American military participation in a European war. Into such a war the Americans have no vital need to enter. Like the English of the past, they are guarded by the ocean, and so long as they maintain sufficient sea and air power, they cannot be seriously hurt. Mr. Truman, as President, may not have believed in the sureness of America's maritime shield, and President Eisenhower appears to be of like mind, but their view of the matter is seriously challenged. In the 1952 Republican campaign for the choice of a Presidential candidate, Senator Taft made no secret of his disapproval of maintaining American troops in Europe or of his confidence that his country could defend itself by ships and aircraft; as Britain did in 1940-44, though her protective moat was only twenty miles wide instead of 3,000. It is therefore very risky for Britons or Frenchmen or West Germans to assume that millions of American soldiers could be counted on for support in a war against Communism. Mr. Dulles would hardly be so ready to threaten the cessation of American aid to Europe if he believed, and thought Europe believed, that America was bound by necessity to provide it.

There are thus two reasons for regarding the North Atlantic Treaty Organisation as a temporary expedient and nothing more; these two reasons being that it militates against the formation of a third group necessary for a balance of power, and that the American keel-plate is insecurely fastened to the rest of the hull and might drop off just when the N.A.T.O. vessel was about to steam into action.

What, then, of this Third Force which we have agreed to be necessary? The most obvious candidate for the post is, of course, Europe. All the main racial stocks of Europe possess intellectual, cultural, and historical heritages which, for all their past squab-blings, are much more closely linked to each other than they are to those of other global regions. It cannot be doubted that they, or some of them, could combine politically without much difficulty. Nor would such a combination create any startling in-novation, since it was first effected over a thousand years ago. Otto's Holy Roman Empire, of which mention was made in Chapter 3, is a precedent of quite respectable antiquity as to what can be done in the way of European combination, comprising as it did the whole of France and Germany and also Hol-land and Belgium. The ancient Holy Roman Empire is therefore a ready-made blueprint, complete with the exceedingly valuable adjuncts of tradition and histor-ical romance, for a European Empire of the present day.

A modern Franco-German combination should present less difficulty than might be thought. Ger-mans who have recently travelled in France refer to the greatest good-will being shown to them by ordi-nary French people, and are convinced of a genuine feeling among them for a reconciliation with their German neighbours. Such Germans speak of friendly enquiries at country garages and *estaminets* by

Frenchmen, who according to the prosecutors at Nuremberg were dragged off to slave labour in Germany during the war, about friends they made in Germany during their slavery. And publicity has recently been given to the case of a Frenchman in Bordeaux who is saving so many francs a month from his wages for the express purpose of paying a visit of friendship to the German slave-master under whom he worked. Such incidents do not indicate an enduring hatred of all Frenchmen for all Germans on the common level. Indeed, M. Jean Giono, in his interview with Mr. Warwick Charlton referred to on page 149 said that the French people's "hatred of the Germans has now been turned against English-speaking foreigners."

The French politicians persist, however, as they persisted before 1939, in a desire to keep Germany down, to have her militarily weak so that France may be secure. They have been and still are using all their endeavours to create a European Army in which the Western Germans shall have a part, but an inferior part only. The French proposals are for a European defence force in which the French and pro-French contingents shall well outnumber the German, while German units are to be brigaded with those of other nationalities and not allowed to be grouped in large homogeneous formations.

It is an attitude which demonstrates that an inability to learn from experience was not a preserve of the Bourbons. The French politicians should know by now that security by repression of stronger rivals does not work. The expedient was tried after 1918 and failed. It failed because it was bound to fail, being against the natural order of things. It was the desperate French attempt to keep Germany permanently disarmed that more than anything else brought Hitler into power and produced the great explosion of 1939, which nearly destroyed European civilisation.

The present French attempt to achieve security by more concealed but similar means will inevitably lead in the same direction as before, and for obvious enough reasons. The Germans, whose unification received its original and main impulse from French ill-usage in Napoleon's time, are now a consciously single nation more numerous than the French, more martial, more efficient, harder working, and more internally co-operative. Napoleon the first is dead and his military glories lie buried with him. Time has marched on and left the French behind; as, in not dissimilar ways, it has also left the British behind.

If there is any wisdom left in them, the French politicians must see that the only sane solution of their problem is for France to fill the central European vacuum in her own favour by burying the hatchet with Germany completely, and making the closest possible accord with the Western Germans for mutual security against the new giant menace from the east. French security *vis-à-vis* Germany should rest on friendship instead of repression. But the French are seeking the impossible. They want a Germany strong enough to keep the Russians at bay but weak enough to cause no tremors to France; and the two are incompatible.

16

Britain and the
Immediate Future

What is the British attitude towards these problems?
It is, in fact, very hesitating and confused. A year
or so ago there was much advocacy of a federation
of Europe, and British politicians of both parties
seemed to be competing for the credit of supporting it
the more ardently. Yet just as the idea began to take
form, with the co-operation of the West European countries, what did Britain do but begin to back out and say
it is none of her business.

Part of the British coyness is probably due to the influence of those who favour a Commonwealth bloc to
which Britain should attach herself rather than to any
European combination. Whether Britain could form an
economic bloc with the Commonwealth countries lies
outside the scope of this book to consider. She certainly
could not form a strategic bloc with them. The com-
ponent parts of the Commonwealth are much too
widely dispersed over the globe to be able to render
each other effective military support, if support were
forthcoming from nowhere else. It is a matter of months

before Australia could send troops to Britain and vice versa, and war has a habit of moving faster than that.

Britain, it is true, has not yet lost the capacity to protect herself by herself against attack, as the years 1940 and 1941 made plain, despite many gloomy pre-war prophecies to the contrary. Yet something more is required if our object of peace for as long as possible is to be attained. What is wanted for that is a strategical unit, of which Britain is a part, that is strong enough to discourage other major powers from trying warlike conclusions with it at all. And such a unit postulates a compact group of nations of the requisite aggregate strength, and also within easy enough reach of each other to enable that strength to be rapidly deployed.

For her associates in forming such a group Britain must look to Europe. It is from the European direc-tion that the most serious threats to her security have previously come and are likely to come again, and it is therefore in that area, too, that she must seek her comrades in arms.

This is not a matter of loyalty or disloyalty to the Commonwealth nations. It is just a question of ge-ography. The Australians and New Zealanders have re-cently acted in this very way in their own Pacific area, when they arranged a pact with the United States from which Britain was excluded. Complaints that have been made in Britain about Dominion acquiescence in that exclusion were ill-advised. For twenty years, be-tween 1921 and 1941, Australia and New Zealand relied on British assurances of succour in time of trouble. Yet when trouble came to them, Britain failed them badly; just as they, in the same crisis, embarrassed the British by insisting, though with perfect reason, on withdraw-ing their own troops from the Mediterranean for the defence of their homeland. Danger close at hand always takes priority over danger farther off. It is therefore a very natural piece of realism for Australia and New Zealand to make separate defence arrangements with another white power in the Pacific, and instead of muttering reproaches the British should follow their example at home.* Nor should the strengthening of Britain's strategical position in Europe prejudice the position of the Commonwealth. On the contrary, it would lessen the likelihood of the Dominions being called upon for further sacrifices for Britain's defence, while they could still adhere, if they wished, to any larger strategical group with which Britain might align herself.

It follows that Britain should throw in her lot with the European "Third Force," the need for which was stated in the last chapter. But although the British Government has made certain gestures in that direction, they have been only half-hearted. Up to the time of writing, Britain has refused to join the European Army plan, confining herself to promising a limited assistance to that army, independently provided.

Moreover, so far as can be judged from the semi-veiled way in which the negotiations regarding European defence are conducted, the British Government seems to be at least a partial subscriber to the doctrine that the French are entitled to safeguards against Germany as well as against Russia, and a full subscriber to the belief that though the West Germans must do their duty in defending Western Europe, their role must be a subordinate one.

In the author's view, these attitudes are quite inconsistent with true statecraft. If the Russian menace is as serious as it is said to be and seems to be, England,

---

* The resolute refusal of the Americans to allow Britain, despite her interests in Malaya, Hong Kong, and Borneo, to participate in the Pacific Conference was quite another matter.

like France, cannot afford to have reservations of any kind about the organisation of defence measures. If one has to pick a friend for a tight corner, one does not, if one has any sense, pick the weakest there is or one that is in a notoriously bad state of health. The French are an indifferent proposition as allies. They were much more of a liability than an asset to us in the First World War. They did not last long in the Second World War. And France's alliance-value is now thought to be very low indeed. There are, of course, the small nations; but these will always suffer militarily from the deficiencies inherent in their size.

If we need really stalwart friends for the business of keeping the Russians at bay, Germany is quite obviously the place to look first for them. The Germans are the toughest fighters in Europe. They are also our own traditional allies, on whose side we fought all through the eighteenth century. We were friendly towards them all through the nineteenth century, after taking with them the principal part in the overthrow of Napoleon in 1815. Only in this twentieth century has there been bad blood between Britain and Germany, and even that has not really been between Briton and German. General Sir Charles Harington, when Governor of Gibraltar, noted how extremely well the ordinary Germans and British got on together when they met under anything like normal conditions. Describing the visit of the German pocket battleship *Deutschland* to Gibraltar with wounded during the Spanish Civil War, the General wrote:

". . . here were our sailors of H.M.S. *Hood* and the sailors of the *Deutschland* going about arm in arm, the greatest of friends, playing football, and visiting cafés and cinemas together. Our sailors will do that with the Germans, for whom they have the greatest respect, *and with no one else."*

Yet any proposal to invite the co-operation of the Germans in Western defence to the fullest extent possible has for years been met by whimpers of apprehension or growls of distaste from all those in Britain whose minds are still dominated by the hatred and fear propaganda of the war years. In speeches and letters to the press, the nervous have been pouring out anxiety lest a new German Army, though recruited initially in aid of the West, might not turn against it later on. One prominent Socialist politician even allowed himself to describe German rearmament of any kind as "an irrevocable stage along the road to hell on earth," an opinion that Wellington would have thought very queer. There is, of course, some hazard in a revival of the German Army. But it is even more certain that to succeed in any important project without taking risks is a vain and futile hope. Something, as Nelson said before Trafalgar, must be left to chance.

It may well be that the modern craze for life-long security has so impregnated the population of Britain as to arouse an automatic resistance to taking risks of any kind. Hence, when presented with the problem of whether to be more frightened of the Russians or the Germans, there has been a marked tendency to meet it, as the French are meeting it, by being equally frightened of both at the same time. But it is a fatal tendency, because if the British at the present time cannot be friends with Russia, they cannot afford not to be friends with Germany.

The attitude of reserve towards the Germans which

* *Tim Harington Looks Back*, John Murray, p. 197. (Present author's italics)

is still all too common in England fits in very well with Napoleon's scornful description of a Council of War, when he wrote:

"The same consequences which have uniformly attended long discussions and councils of war will follow at all times. They will terminate in the adoption of the worst course, which in war is always the most timid, or, if you will, the most prudent. The only true wisdom in a General is determined courage."

Or, it may be added, in a Foreign Secretary. The country that is too fearful of taking risks in its choice of friends will end by having no friends at all, or no friends of real value. Students of naval history, contemplating the tortuous political shufflings of recent years to create a German Army outside German control, will be reminded of the scene in the cabin of the *London* at the Council of War before Copenhagen when Nelson was stamping up and down and declaring that "the boldest course is the safest, depend upon it" in a frantic endeavour to stir up to decisive action a weak and hesitant Commander-in-Chief.

But if we want the Germans as loyal allies, it is quite futile to go on treating them as convicted criminals. Instead, we must make friends with them, which means according them complete and absolute equality of status and removing all sources of friction, annoyance, and resentment. First and foremost, there cannot be too quick an amnesty for the so-called German war criminals. The continued imprisonment of German officers is one of the chief obstacles to a willing association of the fighting stock of Germany with Western defence.*

---

*   A recent Resolution by various German Service and ex-Service Associations is given in Appendix 2.

All Germans who fought in the last war regard the heavy sentences of many of their senior officers not only as monstrous injustices in themselves but as intolerable slurs on the professional honour of the German services. They regard the whole series of the Nuremberg Trials as epoch-making pieces of hypocrisy, which is exactly what they were. To prove that beyond cavil, and without having to go into any other evidence, it is only necessary to mention that the Americans, with British approval, destroyed 80,000 unsuspecting Japanese men, women, and children at Hiroshima (and more at Nagasaki) by the fearful new weapon of the atom bomb, and immediately turned with majestic self-righteousness to try a number of the German leaders for "crimes against humanity." On that score alone, it would be hardly surprising if the Germans think us moral humbugs of Olympic standard.

Then the French must hand back the Saar, to which the recent rigged election gives them no honest right, and which they have only been able to acquire because Germany, to whom they could not stand up by themselves, had been beaten by a combination of three of the greatest powers on earth. The French are the inventors of the subtle argument that Germany should share certain of her material assets with other neighbour nations "for the good of Europe." That argument does not apply only to Germany. When the Germans were in occupation of France, they estimated that French agriculture could be much expanded if more labour and better methods were introduced. An appropriate accompaniment of a German 'pooling' of coal and iron resources would therefore be a settling on French soil of some of the east-German refugees, for the greater production of food from the French countryside to the general benefit of western Europe.

These acts of restitution and conciliation are urgent. In the 1920s and early 1930s the political procrastinators argued away one precious year after another in their endless and fruitless discussions about what should be done about Germany one day. They went on so long, without that day ever coming, that the Germans grew impatient and took the law into their own hands. There is little doubt that they are growing impatient now. While we lengthily debate what degrees of freedom they can have, the chances of their seeking it in a way we should not like grow inevitably greater.

If the French will not forget their grievances against Germany (which are actually no greater than the German grievances against France) and work in closely with her in organising a European "Third Force," Britain should make a pact with the Germans independently. But a triangular arrangement of Britain, France, and Western Germany is preferable, as being more in accord with intelligent realities. These three are the citadel powers of Europe, and if they can come to an understanding, the job is four-fifths done.

Assuming that these three countries could manage to combine strategically, the next question is, should they remain independent politically or should they coalesce politically as well and become one country? I confine the question to the citadel powers because, in my view, too much time should not be spent in trying to work out a perfect, all-embracing system. Britain, West Germany, and France should be able to come to a foundation agreement among themselves much more easily on a tripartite basis than is possible with a comprehensive, multiple plan covering everybody, large and small, down to the last detail. With the central citadel firmly constructed, the adherence of the peripheral countries should be easy enough, or of such as wished to adhere.

Some might not. There are, after all, a good many splinter States on the American continent, dominated though it is by the United States.

The answer to the above question of independent alliances or political combination needs to be sought in relation to our object, that is to say, lasting peace. From that angle, there can surely be little doubt that the right solution is political union. A military alliance of sovereign states can serve to meet a particular emergency, but all history, including recent history, shows that it does not outlast the emergency in question. Therefore, a European Army, composed of national contingents from separate countries, would tend to disintegrate as soon as the Russian menace became, or appeared to become, less urgent. Or it might do so, even before, from internal jealousies. A European Army provided by three or six or nine separate governments would be like a ship with three or six or nine captains, who could be relied upon sooner or later to intrigue against one another for a greater share of power or a lesser share of the hard work or for some other reason.

Nor are these dangers to be avoided by the device of a Supreme Commander. He is not the real captain of the ship, but commands in the full sense only one section of the crew, while any of the others are liable to walk ashore without his permission by order of some outside body. The determining factor is that of responsibility. In a League of Nations, United Nations, N.A.T.O., or similar army, the ultimate responsibility is owed not to the Commander, however Supreme, or to some supranational board or committee, but to the taxpayers who pay for the troops and are therefore in a position to say, through their national government, how the troops shall be used. In the first flush of the Korean war, the separate sets of tax-payers were inclined to overlook that aspect of the U.N. forces in their enthusiasm for an international organisation 'with teeth.' But when the molars failed to grind the opponent into pulp, those who paid for and provided the U.N. contingents began to be more and more aware of their ownership.

Long-term peace depends on long-term military strength, and this demands unity of control, which in turn can only be achieved by political amalgamation. The Roman Empire maintained itself inviolate for hundreds of years because the Roman Legions, although they came from many different races, were all under one authority and were unrivalled in strength and efficiency; and when Rome fell it was primarily from internal decay. The two most secure countries in the world today are the United States of America and the Union of Soviet Socialist Republics. They are more secure than any others precisely because they are stronger; and they are stronger because they are politically unified and strategically autarkic. Split up the 48 states of the North American Union into independent countries and they would be in acute danger at once.

Therefore, and unless we can induce the United States and Russia to undertake a sub-division into a number of smaller and separate sovereignties—which is unlikely—our goal of long-term peace calls for Britain, France, and Western Germany to join forces politically. They could do this by fusion or by interstate federation. That would be a matter of taste. Junction of some kind and political unity in foreign policy and defence are the basic requirements.

The same considerations serve to indicate why a British-European combination is preferable to a

British-American association. For the Americans, the latter is a temporary convenience but not an essential. Should anything happen to lessen the Russian danger, the United States' need of Britain would greatly diminish and she might easily be cast adrift. But a junction of Britain, France, and Western Germany would have the stability deriving from their common interest in permanent association if they are again to enjoy the independence and wield the influence in the world to which their talents and characters entitle them. Neither Britain nor Germany nor France can now be a great power without the collaboration of the other two. The United States is a great power already, with or without British or European support. Britain and France and Western Germany are each secondary powers and can only regain a position of first-class importance in partnership.

It is a matter of considerable interest that Hitler, a European, took a broader and more sympathetic view of the British Empire than did President Roosevelt, an American. It has already been mentioned that there is apparently convincing evidence to the effect that the German dictator not only did not want to see that Empire broken up but regarded it as a beneficent world institution which ought to be preserved. We are, however, indebted to Mr. Elliott Roosevelt's book on his father's wartime conversations, of which the son was an ear-witness, for making it plain that the President took the opposite view and worked consistently to give it effect.* We are therefore presented with the extraordinary paradox that Britain's principal enemy was anxious for the British Empire to remain in being, while her princi-

* *As He Saw It*, Duell, Sloan & Pearce, N.Y., p. 25.

pal ally, the United States, was determined to destroy it.

The policy of keeping Britain outside the European Army organisation and clear of European political combinations appears to take no account of changed world conditions. It was a quite feasible policy for Britain to hold aloof from Europe in the nineteenth century; for at that time commercial expansion in the overseas world was hers for the asking, due to the generally undeveloped state of the globe on the one hand and, on the other, to the fact that Britain then possessed the world's supreme navy and the geographical position *vis-à-vis* her chief rivals to use it to the greatest effect. Now, in the mid-twentieth century, these conditions favourable to an extra-European policy have largely disappeared. World markets for British trade no longer offer prospects of indefinite expansion, and Britain has lost not only her large foreign investments but also the primary asset for the secure exploitation of what markets there are—her superior sea power. Her navy is now the second and not the first in the world. Strategically, she enjoys her overseas markets by permission of the United States.

As things are, it seems to me the plainest folly for Britain to support the principle of a unified Europe in which she is not a full partner. For were such unification to become an accomplished fact, Britain would be left as a weak buffer state between the two large aggregations of power represented by the United States of Europe and of America; a kind of insular Alsace-Lorraine whose ownership the two adjacent giants would be almost certain to dispute.

Moreover, if Britain really wants Europe to be successful as a new power group, she has an indispensable contribution to make to that end. She must use her fleet to keep European waters secure for Europe's benefit. For two centuries she has done the opposite. Every attempt to unify Europe, from Louis XIV to Adolf Hitler, has been thwarted by the hostile pressure of British sea power. If, now, frustration is to be changed to promotion, the role of the British Navy must change too. It must become Europe's maritime guardian instead of its besieger.

An Anglo-French-Western German Union would, I venture to hope, provide a cure, and the only likely cure, for certain maladies at present affecting all three of the potential partners. For Britain it would offer the chance of the early removal of that internal growth, which may at any moment prove to be a malignant growth, of military occupation by a foreign power. For France, it might be, by the elimination of the neurosis of a German danger, the road to returning health and national rejuvenation. And, for Germany, it offers what is probably the best chance of a solution of the burning problem of the national division between Communism and the West. At heart, the Germans are Westerners and not pro-Russians, and only harshly uncompromising treatment by the Atlantic nations could make them turn eastward. A firm union of Britain, France, and Western Germany, on terms of *absolutely equal partnership,* should act as so powerful a magnet to the Eastern Germans as to secure that these latter would take the earliest practicable opportunity of falling into place alongside their West German compatriots, and should render any Russian attempt to use an Eastern German Army against the West too dangerous to be tried.

I have, moreover, a strong feeling that the march of events in Britain has introduced subtle alterations in the national psychology; in particular, that a point of overcrowding has now been reached that is causing a species of collective claustrophobia. For their mental health, the English have always needed an open-air life, plenty of room, and comparative freedom to live their own lives in their own way. These conditions they have now very largely lost. They are compressed into industrial towns, shut off from nature, faced with increasing regimentation, including the recently established bugbear of conscription and the recurring threat of direction of labour, while most of them are virtually forced to pay tribute to some organization which they may or may not like in order to get work. Overshadowing their future is the terrible dilemma that an increasing population in a country which cannot feed itself is bound to make a dangerous situation get steadily worse, as more and more houses are built at the expense of more and more agricultural land to accommodate more and more people who can live only by insecure dependence on treacherous foreign markets. There is reason to think that the tight little island of Britain has become too tight, so that there has arisen an instinctive impulse for an expansion of physical, spiritual, and political horizons. There are few post-war restrictions that are so much disliked and considered so irksome as those on travel to the continent of Europe, with its promise of escape from the England of rules, regulations, rations, and satellite towns.

Popular instinct in this respect is doubtless affected, although unconsciously, by the epochal development of this generation—the break-up of the British Empire. Under the first Queen Elizabeth, the maritime English sallied forth to seek fortune and adventure overseas, with the ultimate result that the flag of Britain came to fly on every continent of the globe. Now, four centuries later and under the second Elizabeth, the process has gone into reverse. The flag has been struck in one part of the world after another and the sceptre of Empire has been given over to other hands. India, Burma, and Ceylon have gone. Malaya has been promised its independence, and mischief-making British busybodies are hard at work goading British Africa into another Boston Tea Party, while the already independent Dominions are steadily loosening their ties with the Mother Country and transferring their affections in other directions.

The native British, though I do not think they fully realise it yet, are being forced back to a closer and closer scrutiny of their immediate surroundings. They can no longer seek their salvation across the seas but must look for it near at hand; that is, on the continent of Europe.

17

Conclusions

Now to summarise the major conclusions reached. It is first of all a dangerous delusion to suppose that war can be banished from the world altogether. There are some issues between nations which are incapable of solution except by a trial of strength, such an issue being the Franco-Prussian quarrel of 1870 when both sides thought they could gain the same object, the leadership of Europe, by force—and one was wrong.

The world is in a state of continuous change. Like individuals and families, nations and Empires rise in importance and also decline; and when either process occurs there seems to be no way of allowing for expansion in the one case or of apportioning the inheritance in the other except by what is called power politics; or, to put it in plainer language, by the power of the sword, in which the strongest comes off best. Even though the Jews were presented with a country by vote of the United Nations, they had to fight to keep it and may well have to fight again. And among the numerous causes of the First World

War, one of the most fundamental was the gradual decay of the Turkish Empire, which opened a wider and wider door to competitive ambitions among the Balkan Slavs, the Russians, and the Austrians. The Yugo-Slav movement of the early years of this century was the natural outcome of the weakening of the Turk, whose own earlier invasions of south-east Europe had originally been due to the enfeeblement of the Eastern Roman Empire. Hence, the implied assumption behind the United Nations' attitude in condemnation of aggression—that the world can be permanently stabilised on its present political basis— is on a par with commanding the sun to stand still in the heavens.

But though wars may have to be, it is a pity to make them more savage, more frequent, and more universal than is necessary, which is clearly what has been happening during this twentieth century. What has been wrong about these recent wars? Primarily the widespread and basic misconception of what is the purpose of the whole business. The modern idea, manifested on two major occasions, that once a war has begun it must engulf the whole world and go on until one side or the other has been knocked prostrate in order to gain what is called victory is as fantastic as to say that every lawsuit, no matter what about, should go on until one of the litigants is ruined. Where is the victory that the British are said to have gained over Germany? What does it avail them to say that German militarism has been overthrown when they themselves are now subjected to military conscription for the first time during peace, except for a few months in 1939; or that they have forces helping to occupy Germany when, as members of those forces admit, the Germans are treating them with arrogant disdain, the German people are far better fed than the home population of the victorious British, and the German economy is making far rapider strides towards recovery? Some victory, as Mr. Churchill might have said to the American Senate, had he been more farseeing.

Is America's victory any more impressive? Not much. She is forced to maintain far costlier military establishments than before the war for Germany's defeat, and her people are being heavily taxed in order that her wealth may be poured out to subsidise West European armaments. And why? Precisely because her President Roosevelt's policy of the unconditional surrender of Germany created a military vacuum in Central Europe which was promptly filled in a way that the President had not, though he might have, apprehended. Complete victory has proved an empty triumph for both Britain and the U.S.A.

These lamentably unsatisfactory outcomes of an apparently successful war are attributable to one principal cause—to the pronounced partiality of democratic politicians for basing military strategy on oratorical slogans instead of on established principles formulated by experts. Seldom, if ever, do the politicians at war seem to ask themselves the key questions: What exactly is our political object? Is it a good object in the light of history? Is it attainable? Have we the resources to attain it?

Britain's object in the last war was ill-chosen from the start, being beyond her strength both before and after Mr. Churchill became Prime Minister. And President Roosevelt's and Mr. Churchill's common object of unconditional surrender was faulty because neither of them had the vision to see around the turn of the road of military victory. The nearest that either

of them came to having a political object, the extirpation of Nazi tyranny, was unsound for the reasons
that it was incapable of more than temporary achievement and was a domestic matter of the Germans
with which the democracies had no business to inter-
fere. Its basic unwisdom has recently been emphasised
when, in order to justify a guarantee to the tyrannical
and communistic Marshal Tito, the British authorities
were compelled to declare that disapproval of another
country's internal political system was no bar to an
understanding with it.

Unconditional surrender is a sound enough *military* object if the political object be annihilation or
permanent conquest. But if the enemy of the moment
be contemplated as a post-war neighbour, the expe-
diency of his unconditional surrender becomes much
more questionable. For unconditional surrender is not
only vastly humiliating in itself but lays the vanquished
open to the severest handling by the victors, who, once
having got a powerful enemy down, nowadays seem
fatally addicted to the attempt to keep him down indefinitely. The defeated nation is thus given a first-class
incentive to recover its independent freedom and turn
the tables on its conquerors at the earliest opportunity,
if necessary in blood. The first essential, if you wish to
live in peace and amity with a nation, is not to attack
its self-respect. The greater a people's degradation at
the hands of its enemies, the deeper and more lasting its
resentment and the stronger its eventual reaction. The
forced admission of German war guilt in the Treaty
of Versailles would have been a colossal political
blunder even if it had been true: and it was not true.
The Nuremberg trials were a greater blunder still.

Therefore, in dealing with an enemy who is one of
the major nations of the world, unconditional sur-

render is an object to be approached with reluctance and carried through with moderation and generosity, while a negotiated peace is generally preferable. Even towards a secondary country like Denmark, Nelson (who of all men can hardly be called an appeaser or pamperer) went out of his way to seek the latter solution during the battle of Copenhagen in 1801, sending ashore a conciliatory message and a suggestion for a parley. The suggestion was accepted and led to an agreed settlement. Nowadays, the city of Copenhagen would no doubt be laid flat by bombing and unconditional surrender insisted on.

No fault can be found with General Grant for adopting unconditional surrender as his object in the American Civil War, since it was his Government's known intention to destroy the newly-declared Southern Confederation and reincorporate the southern States in the American Union. But President Roosevelt tried to apply the Grant formula to the very different circumstances of a German war, presumably without realising how dissimilar the two cases were and therefore how the treatment suitable for the one might be disastrously wrong for the other.

As we have seen, the primary consideration in deciding whether to make war should be whether or not the country's *vital interests* require its participation. On this basis, Britain should have kept out of both world wars as she had successfully kept out of the Franco-Prussian war of 1870, her vital interests being involved neither in 1914 nor 1939. Indeed, Sir Edward Grey's 1914 object of preventing Britain being hated, despised, and so on, was about as poor a reason for taking his country into war as could be imagined. There was, of course, the last-minute episode of the German invasion of Belgium, which gave the British

Government a good rallying-cry for a war on which it had already decided for other reasons. Lowes Dickenson quotes British press articles of 1887, thought to be officially inspired at a time when France and Germany were close to war and Britain was more friendly with Germany than with France, arguing that Britain's duty under the Belgian guarantee required her only to ensure that Belgian territory was left intact *after* a war.*

Certain post-1918 propagandists, it is true, contended that Britain had to enter the First World War in order to safeguard the French Channel ports, the loss of which they declared (as Haldane and Grey had also thought) would have been fatal to Britain. The Second World War, in which those ports were actually lost, showed this supposition to be fallacious, as the author predicted would be the case both before the war and in a book he published in 1940 at the height of the Channel ports scare.†

So, too, Britain could have held aloof from the Second World War, which indeed might never have come about but for the inane Polish guarantee—that guarantee which, by making Britain's position clear, was to frighten the German bully from warlike courses. But the scarecrow failed to scare and Britain became embroiled.

Had Britain's *vital interests* really been consulted on both these occasions, she would have been kept free from these hostilities if in any way possible. The British, alone among the Great Powers, had by the twentieth century ceased to be able to feed themselves from their own soil and were dependent for their standard of living and general economic position on large accu-

---

* *The International Anarchy*—Allen & Unwin, p. 30.

† *Sea Power*—Cape (London) and Doubleday Doran (New York), Chapter III.

mulated foreign investments and an established trading reputation. For Britain to liquidate these vitally important commercial assets by entering not one but two ruinously expensive major wars from which she could safely have abstained was therefore strategical and political lunacy, especially as her chief commercial rival, Germany, was involved on both occasions.

Even, moreover, though the politicians took Britain into both world wars, they could and should—if they had known their business—have followed the cheapest way of attaining the national object; cheapest both in blood and material expenditure. By "cheapest" I do not mean a cheeseparing policy whereby Treasury control keeps the fighting services short of arms, as so often in the past. I mean a strategy of the greatest return for the least expenditure, consistent with the object in view.

The object at the back, if not the front, of Sir Edward Grey's mind in 1914 was presumably the preservation of the balance of power. If so, Britain might by an intelligent use of her favourable island position have limited her own effort and Europe's martyrdom at the same time. Instead of planning and working for total victory, she could have offered a return of the captured German colonies if the Germans would agree to evacuate France and make peace on the basis of the *status quo ante.**

But the captured colonies were not regarded as bargaining counters but as booty. Greed ousted honour, and the initial declaration by the Prime Minister that Britain sought no territorial aggrandisement for herself was conveniently forgotten. The colonies were retained, and Britain went on to gain complete victory

---

* The Germans made an offer of peace in December, 1916, on almost these lines, but the Allies refused to consider it.

at the expense of a million Imperial dead and crippling financial expenditure.

As for the balance of power, it died the death; the intoxication of complete victory leading the victors to destroy the balance by eliminating the Austrian Empire, limiting Germany's military strength, and handing over the hegemony of Europe to France. The same policy of unbalance was again resorted to in 1945 in an even more extreme form and with even more unfortunate results.

In the Second War, Mr. Churchill had several opportunities for choosing a relatively economical way of pursuing the basic national interest of security, but instead he preferred the path of unsparing and indeed reckless prodigality. Britain's quarrel with Germany was allegedly over the Nazi dictatorship. Therefore, when Germany proceeded to attack another dictator country, Mr. Churchill was presented with a good opportunity, if he had held a statesmanlike view of the war, to disengage his country and mark time belligerently so as to allow the German and Russian tyrannies to knock each other to pieces at no loss to Britain. And even had Germany knocked Russia out, it was surely a reasonable estimate that the former would for years have been too busy organising her new eastern *lebensraum* to bother about an attack on Britain, which anyway had not come off even under the specially favourable conditions of 1940. It has, moreover, been previously argued that, even as things were, Mr. Churchill could advantageously have considered coming to terms with Germany in the later stages of the war.

But Mr. Churchill was not a statesman seeking always his own country's advantage amid the twists and turns of a dangerous world. He was an international crusader preaching and conducting a holy war for the destruction of the Hitler régime and the German military power at any cost; at any cost to his own country and the rest of the world. In his own words, there was no sacrifice he would not make to get rid of Hitler, although up to the British declaration of war against Germany in 1939 Hitler had done no harm to Britain and had actually gone out of his way to placate her at some sacrifice to German pride by agreeing to keep the German fleet at a third of the strength of the British. Mr. Churchill's war policy was not national but religious.

So was President Roosevelt's. We have that revealing interview between Mr. Hopkins and Mr. Churchill mentioned in Chapter 7, when the latter described his American visitor as "absolutely glowing with refined comprehension of the Cause.* It was to be the defeat, ruin, and slaughter of Hitler, to the exclusion of all other purposes, loyalties, and aims." To the exclusion, for instance, of the fact that the United States was not at war with Germany, that Germany had done her, too, no harm, and that Mr. Hopkins' master had just been telling American mothers "again and again and again" that their sons would not be sent to fight in Europe. Mr. Churchill thus shows that President Roosevelt's attitude towards the war had little if any relation to American interests. The President, like the British Prime Minister, was a crusader.

Leading Americans have, in fact, been almost more neglectful of the principle of vital interests than their British counterparts. The United States had need to enter neither of the last two wars as a major

---

* "Refined" seems to the author a singular choice of adjective in this context.

belligerent against Germany, despite Germany's declaration of war against her on the second occasion; for
in neither case did America's vital interests demand
Germany's complete overthrow.* Since the American
quarrel with Germany in 1917 was about the U-boat
warfare, hostilities could have been confined to the
ocean, as was the case between the English and the
Dutch in the seventeenth century. In the Anglo-Dutch
wars the two belligerents were content sometimes just
to convoy their merchant fleets clear of danger, and
sometimes to seek a maritime decision by naval battle.
But neither thought in terms of military invasion or
total victory.

One of the strangest phenomena of our time is the
refusal of the United States to believe in its own en-
viable safety. It is, in truth, one of the least vulnerable
nations of history. With the biggest navy and air
force in the world, with ample man power and boun-
tiful supplies of all the most important raw materials,
with an unrivalled industrial productivity, and
guarded by thousands of miles of ocean on both sides.
Americans can afford to sit tight and watch other
people's squabbles with an amused detachment and
economical advantage.

Instead, they are addicted to conjuring up dangers
which are mainly or totally imaginary as a reason
for entering the fray. Thus, during the last war, President Roosevelt declared that American participation in it was essential in order to save America from
invasion by preventing the Germans from reaching
West Africa. Should they get there, he said, they
could hop across to Brazil or Mexico and march on

---

* The security of the American financial loans to the Entente countries
  would have been better served by a compromise peace in 1917 than by
  a German collapse in 1918.

the United States from the south. With the command of the Atlantic firmly in American hands, the President's estimate of what might happen was ridiculous, and would have meant certain failure to any midshipman in his examinations.

General MacArthur similarly distinguished himself by telling a Senate Committee in 1951 that the United States would "practically lose the Pacific Ocean if Formosa passed into Communist hands"; which latter event would put the west coast of America in "mortal danger."* As the Chinese Communists had and have no fleet to speak of, the naval officer can only stand stupefied by such an opinion expressed by a man who, as Supreme Commander, had a leading say in the United Nations' Far Eastern strategy. The coast of America would only be in mortal danger from a Communist Formosa if Communist Chinese soldiers were able to swim fully equipped under water for 6,000 miles.

One of the most striking manifestations of the American vulnerability complex is the fear of being atom bombed, which, by all accounts, seems to have the nation in its grip. That the United States is immune from such bombing no one would be so foolish as to say. But it is as certain as anything can be that the country will not be defeated by such means.

In support of the opinion the author expressed on this point in Chapter 12, he can quote the late Admiral Sir Herbert Richmond, who said before the war that:

'short cuts to victory, attempts aimed at the final objective, have an almost unbroken record of failure. The doctrine of

* "The Times"—May 5th, 1951.

victory by evasion, direct attack upon the people's life without overcoming their armed forces, can find no support in the experience of war. It is a theory only, yet to be proved.'

It has still to be proved. Nothing that has occurred since the Admiral wrote the above has negatived his judgment. Aerial bombing in the Second World War was not decisive in Europe, where its effect, as the United States Strategic Bombing Survey makes plain, was a great deal less than was prophesied beforehand or than was claimed to be by the air force propagandists at the time it was going on. Nor was it decisive in the Japanese war, for the Japanese Navy had already been defeated and, as a consequence, the Japanese Air Force was grounded through lack of petrol and the country was rendered almost defenceless against air attack before the atom bombs were exploded.

It has been just the same in the Korean war, where air bombing has given notably unimpressive results; for in spite of ceaseless bombing by U.N. aircraft, the North Koreans and Chinese were able up to the armistice to mount heavy attacks on the U.N. troops near the 38th Parallel. Yet the familiar propaganda about the decisiveness of air bombing still goes on with bland disregard of the evidence. Thus on December 3, 1952, a British Air Vice Marshal was reported as saying that "our unchallenged air power dominates the military situation in Korea and will continue to dominate it."*

Just a year earlier, Mr. Hanson W. Baldwin, military correspondent in Korea of the *New York Times*, reported an exactly opposite state of affairs. Commenting on the obvious failure of the many months

* "Times," 3rd December, 1952.

of constant bombing attacks on enemy communications, he said that "we have deluded ourselves— or rather the over-enthusiastic advocates of air power have deluded us. Hundreds of sorties daily against supply lines means nothing: it is hits that count. Many of our sorties . . . are entirely wasted. We miss hitting any important targets." * Mr. Baldwin added that it was the ground forces, not air power, that had been the dominant arm in Korea and was likely to remain so everywhere.

In January of 1953, General Bradley, Chairman of the Joint Chiefs of Staff in Washington, expressed the same opinion when he referred to "the dangerous hope" on the part of many people that the atomic bomb alone could win a war, adding that this hope was fallacious.†

That the bomb has fearful power no one can doubt. It does not follow that its power will be exerted at the right spot. It may never reach that spot, although many people unthinkingly assume that it is bound to. A point never to be forgotten in strategical matters is that the defence is constantly chasing the offence and sometimes outstrips it. Great and formidable as is the secrecy surrounding atomic warfare, enough scraps of information reach the outer world to suggest that the development of the guided missile and the atomic rocket may be transforming the situation in favour of the defence, and to invite the conjecture that against a technically advanced enemy the atom bomb might be a grievous disappointment to its devotees.

The former strong American instinct for the strict avoidance of foreign entanglements seems to have given place to the almost opposite urge for the

* "Times," 3rd December, 1951.

† "Times," 12th January, 1953.

United States to push its way into any outside
trouble wherever in the world it may occur. Thus,
although American troops are garrisoning Europe
and campaigning in Korea, there seems to be an
anxiety in American governmental quarters for them
to be fighting in Indo-China and Malaya as well. But
it is hard to see what vital American interests require
such action in the latter areas; or, for that matter, in
Korea either.

It cannot be over-emphasised that national interests are the only valid factors to justify going to
war. Unfortunately, once involved in any war, even
a cold war, democratic politicians tend to get carried
away by idealistic rhetoric which turns them into
champions of humanity and world reformers. World
reform is, however, the very worst of all objects to be
sought by war. For major war never makes the world
better but always worse. Therefore to seek the "bet-
terment of the common man" and such-like beatific
concepts by getting masses of common men, women
and children killed, maimed, and rendered homeless
is nonsensical.

That is one reason why the slogan often heard
since 1939 that nations have a duty to fight for this
or that cause is so deplorable. No country has a
natural duty to fight anywhere or to kill anybody. If
there is any moral duty at all in this connection, it is
not to fight and not to kill. Every country that keeps
out of a world war is a country saved for peace and
civilisation. If enough keep out, a world war ceases
to be such but dwindles into a localised conflict, and
a localised war is less dangerous than a general one
precisely because there is a substantial body of non-
belligerents who can take a detached and temperate,
if not actually impartial, view of the quarrel, and

whose influence may therefore be useful in discouraging belligerent extremism. That is why it is an international misfortune that Americans seem incapable of realising the strategical blessings that Providence has bestowed on them. They are the natural neutrals of the world and therefore, by reason of their strength, the ideal arbitrators between outside disputants. But they cannot fulfil this beneficial function if they are always dreading attack from foreigners who cannot effectively reach them, and therefore keep on becoming active partisans of one side or another.

But Mr. Churchill also appears to be no believer in the merits of localising conflict. At the time of Marshal Tito's visit to London in March 1953, official communiqués issued from Downing Street stated categorically that a war in which Jugoslavia was involved could not be localised. On his return to Belgrade, the Marshal stated that Mr. Churchill had told him, "we are your allies, and if Jugoslavia is attacked we shall fight and die together." Mr. Churchill, speaking several days after this had appeared in print, did not dissent from it.

It is a sombre indication of the dull lassitude that seems to have overspread the British mind in regard to foreign affairs that this startling revelation that Britain had given another of those guarantees of lamentable record to a far-distant country evoked practically no comment either in Parliament or elsewhere. Before the First World War, Sir Edward Grey had not dared to acknowledge the ties which he knew were binding his country to the support of the French. Writing to the British Ambassador in Paris in 1912, he said: "there would be a row in Parliament here if I used words which implied the possibility of a secret engagement . . . committing us to a European war." There was no row in Parliament when Mr. Churchill announced a British commitment to defend Jugoslavia to the death.

Why, however, should it have been assumed that a Russian attack on Jugoslavia could not be localised? The Russian absorption of Czecho-Slovakia had been localised. So had a number of modern wars, including the Franco-Prussian war of 1870, the Anglo-Boer war of 1899, the Russo-Japanese war of 1904, the Balkan wars of 1912, and the Indian-Hyderabad war of 1949. If localisation was possible in these cases, why should it be impossible in that of Jugoslavia?

No doubt a certain amount of sentimental sympathy could be worked up in Britain for "little Jugoslavia" were she to become involved in a struggle with the "big Russian bully," even though it would be a case of one Communist state attacking another, and though Britain has not infrequently acted the part of big bully herself. But sentiment by itself is no adequate reason for embarking on war, as Queen Victoria exemplified when she frustrated Lord Palmerston's endeavor to rush into war against Austria and Prussia in support of "little Denmark" in 1864; in taking which stand the Queen postponed a general European war by fifty years.

As we have seen, and as Queen Victoria insisted on the above occasion, a Government ought to decide on war only in pursuit of its own country's *vital* interests. What vital British interests, therefore, are involved in the defence of Jugoslavia against Russia? A Russian conquest of Tito's country would take Russian power no further west than it is at present. It might, however, be argued that, Jugoslavia being a vital bastion of anti-Russianism in south-east Europe, its fall would lead to Constantinople and the famous waterways of the Bosphorus and Dardanelles passing into Russian hands, and the great bogey, to so many British minds in the last century, of free Russian access to the Mediterranean becoming a fact.

But not surely to Mr. Churchill's mind. The curious thing about that bogey is that it apparently lost its terror during the First World War, when the British Government of 1915 promised Constantinople and the Straits to Russia, and only went back on the promise because Russia made a separate peace. And the point to be specially noted about this promise is that it was made by a Government of which Mr. Churchill was a member. Not only that, but he was the prime instigator of the Dardanelles expedition of 1915 to open the Straits for Russia's benefit.

If, therefore, the exclusion of Russia from the Mediterranean was not vital then, why should it be now? The chief claimant to vital British interest in that sea has traditionally been the shipping route through the Suez Canal. The preservation of this "Imperial life-line" has often been declared essential to British survival, there being many instances of this declaration in the years of tension just before the war of 1939. But when the "life-line" was actually cut for the three years from 1940 to 1943, during which time the Imperial communications had to pass round the Cape, the extra distance turned out to be inconvenient but not fatal. The Suez route was not vital after all.

It is still less vital now that India and Burma have passed outside British control. The route to India is no longer Imperial; and the routes to Australia and New Zealand are only a small fraction lengthier round the Cape than by the Canal. On examination, in fact, there seems to be no imperative reason why Britain should be inevitably drawn into a Jugoslav war and therefore, from her point of view, why such a war could not be localised. But perhaps there are more obscure factors in the case; though, if so, the British public which will have to do the dying ought to have some idea of what they are. In the light of the fearful price paid for the commitment to France before 1914, and the guarantee to Poland in 1939, it appears very strange that Parliament had no questions to ask about the guarantee to Jugoslavia in 1953.

Some of the greatest of the British statesmen of the nineteenth century were thoroughly hostile to the "guarantee" principle. Both Salisbury and Gladstone were agreed that "England should keep entire in her own hands the means of estimating her own obligations upon the various states of facts *as they arise* . . . England should not foreclose and narrow her own liberty of choice by declarations made to the Powers in their real or supposed interests of which they would claim to be joint interpreters . . . England, come what may, should promise too little rather than too much."* In other words, wait till the crisis comes before you decide how to react to it, and do not allow, by committing yourself in advance, your national fate to be determined by foreigners. It is a precept which to the author seems charged with wisdom. Britain was dragged into war in 1914 by French and Russian policies over which she had next to no control, in 1939 by the action of Polish politicians, and in 1941 against Japan by American policies to which the British Prime Minister had publicly given a blank cheque.

As important as anything in relation to the problem of warfare is the handling of the evidence. Inaccurate data do not make for sound conclusions. Yet the modern politicians' surrender to the lure of propaganda is so complete that they make no serious attempt to present the data with faithful objectivity to

* Algernon Cecil—*Queen Victoria and Her Prime Ministers,* p. 338.

warring peoples. Far from it. They set about doctoring the evidence in the most brazen fashion. The flood of distortions, half-truths, and plain fairy-tales about the enemy which are passed into wartime circulation are well-suited to stimulate hatred but are inimical to any cool appraisement by the people of the rights and wrongs of the situation and therefore to the formation of any sound and reliable public judgment as to where the true national interest lies in relation thereto.

Twin brother to the hatred propaganda is the Innocence Line which the politicians, abetted by 'patriotic' historians and international lawyers, draw through past and present events. Every aggression, act of brigandage, or piece of savagery on the home side of the line is labelled as part of "the great historic processes" of human development or a legitimate act of reprisal or some such saving term. But the same things on the enemy side become monstrous crimes against peace and humanity punishable by death.

To give just one example; it will be remembered what a hullabaloo was made in Britain about the wicked German aggression against Norway in 1940. At Nuremberg in 1946 the German Grand Admiral Raeder was accused of participating in that aggression and was given the fearful sentence of imprisonment for life—that is, he was sentenced to die in prison. But the publication in 1952 of the Official British History of the Norwegian Campaign has revealed the shaming fact that plans had been prepared as early as November 1939 for an Anglo-French invasion of Norway under cover of helping the Finns against the Russians; and those plans were not put into operation only because the Russo-Finnish war came to an unexpectedly early end before all was ready.

The Innocence Line is a most valuable expedient for victors bent on vengeance and for propagandists peddling hatred, but it does an ill service to peace by presenting history in masquerade dress and obscuring the stark underlying truth that all nations are basically as bad as each other and that aggression is properly to be regarded as a continuous process reaching back to Cain and Abel. If the victorious nations who have so recently condemned so-called aggression as criminal were conscientiously to search their own history with a view to obeying the laws they themselves made at Nuremberg, the Americans would have to pack up their traps and return to Europe, and the English to Denmark and—strangely enough—to Germany.

To invite men to believe that all their troubles are due to some foreigner's evil eye is a piece of intellectual deceptionism calculated to confuse and mislead the common people of the world to their own detriment. The only sure way to combat disease of any kind is resolutely to trace it to its true sources, and if one of the clues points towards one's own drainage system or water supply or way of living, no amount of burning of sorcerers in the market place will effect a cure. Nations falsely convinced by propaganda of their own immaculate purity are easily persuaded to the idea that they are instruments of the divine justice with the duty of scourging the wicked; a dangerous state of mind conducive to fanatical hatred and so to the excessive brutality for which religious wars are noted. It is also a natural development for nations believing themselves to be the Lord's Anointed to argue that if they will only combine as the guardians of international virtue, peace can be assured for ever. The fantastic result is a call for universal war whenever the most trifling dispute erupts into violence. Instead of taking the attitude that the police adopt in cases of civil disturbances of 'keep out of this,' the United Nations' call is for everyone to come in. Thus, the present-day world is presented with the vista of distant and receding peace to be reached through universal and perpetual war.

It is true that the most insignificant quarrel can be represented as of global concern, just as every minor factory dispute could with equal logic be made a reason for calling a general strike. But the experience of 1926 seems to have convinced British Trade Unionism that a policy of isolation of trouble is to be preferred to unlimited 'sympathetic' support.

This is not to say that there are not evil politicians in the world, whose behaviour can be regarded as reprehensibly unpleasant. But they are never quite as evil as their never entirely innocent accusers make them out to be, and they may and often do have a better case for their conduct than the opposition nations know, or, rather, are allowed to know. The only sound foreign attitude towards such politicians is to leave their moral worth to the people to whom they are responsible, and confine one's active disapproval to any threatened or actual impingement on one's own interests. To extirpate by force all the wicked politicians there are in the world, just because they are wicked, is beyond human accomplishment, the supply being apparently inexhaustible and the number of fully qualified and certificated extirpators being somewhat rare. Moral indignation at another nation's expense is nearly always injudicious. Kaiser Wilhelm's scorn over Britain's behaviour to the Boers was soon returned sevenfold over the German violation of Belgian neutrality, while the recent sanguinary episodes in U.N. Korean prisoner-of-war camps were not a happy aftermath to numerous executions of Germans by the victors in the war for much the same thing.

If the ways of the world are to be improved, it will be by example and not by atomic fission, jellied petrol, rockets, doodle-bugs, or bacteriological bouquets. When any nation has succeeded in getting its own affairs undeviatingly on to the straight and narrow path of righteousness, it will then be entitled to turn its critical attention to the internal conduct of its neighbours. But something tells me that that time is a long way off for any of us, and meanwhile there is plenty for all of us to do at home.

I will end by quoting a letter from Sidney Smith to Lady Grey, wife of the Prime Minister in the 1830s. Though written over a hundred years ago, the letter could as suitably have been composed today.

"For God's sake, do not drag me into another war! I am worn down and worn out, with crusading and defending Europe, and protecting mankind: I *must* think a little of myself. I am sorry for the Spaniards—I am sorry for the Greeks—I deplore the fate of the Jews; the people of the Sandwich Islands are groaning under the most detestable tyranny; Bagdad is oppressed; I do not like the present state of the Delta; Thibet is not comfortable. Am I to fight for all these people? The world is bursting with sin and sorrow. Am I to be Champion of the Decalogue, and to be eternally raising fleets and armies to make all men good and happy? We have just done saving Europe, and I am afraid the consequence will be that we shall cut each others' throats. No war, dear Lady Grey!—No eloquence, but apathy, selfishness, common sense, arithmetic! I beseech you, secure Lord Grey's swords and pistols, as the housekeeper did Don Quixote's armour."

Appendix

I

THE EMS TELEGRAM AND BISMARCK'S PRESS COMMUNIQUÉ

The Ems Telegram as sent by the King of Prussia:

"His Majesty writes to me: 'Count Benedetti spoke to me on the promenade, in order to demand from me, finally in a very importunate manner, that I should authorise him to telegraph at once that I bound myself for all future time never again to give my consent if the Hohenzollerns should renew their candidature. I refused at last somewhat sternly as it is neither right nor possible to undertake engagements of this kind à tout jamais. I told him that I had as yet received no news, and as he was earlier informed from Paris and Madrid than myself, he could see clearly that my Government had no more interest in the matter.' His Majesty has since received a letter from Prince Charles Anthony. His Majesty having told Count Benedetti that he was awaiting news from the Prince, has decided, with reference to the above demand, on the suggestion of Count Eulenberg and myself, not to receive Count Benedetti again, but only to let him be informed through an aide-de-camp: 'That his Majesty has now received from the Prince confirmation of the news which Benedetti had already received from Paris, and had nothing further to say to the Ambassador.' His Majesty leaves it to your Excellency to decide whether Benedetti's fresh demand and its rejection should be at once communicated both to our ambassadors abroad and to the Press."

As issued by Bismarck to the Press:

"After the news of the renunciation of the hereditary Prince of Hohenzollern had been officially communicated to the Imperial Government of France by the Royal Government of Spain, the French Ambassador further demanded of his Majesty, the King, at Ems, that he would authorise him to telegraph to Paris that his Majesty, the King, bound himself for all time never again to give his consent should the Hohen-zollerns renew their candidature. His Majesty, the King, there-upon decided not to receive the French Ambassador again, and sent the aide-de-camp on duty to tell him that his Majesty had nothing further to communicate to the Ambassador."

II

THE AUSTRIAN DEMANDS ON SERBIA
IN 1914

1   Suppression of anti-Austrian publications.
2   Dissolution of a named anti-Austrian propaganda society.
3   Elimination from public instruction of anti-Austrian propaganda.
4   Removal from the Government service of all officers and functionaries guilty of such propaganda, the Austrian Government to supply the names.
5   Serbia to accept the collaboration in Serbia of representatives of the Austro-Hungarian Government for the suppression of the subversive movement directed against the territorial integrity of the monarchy.
6   Serbia to take judicial proceedings against accessories to the plot of the 28th June (assassination) who are on Serbian territory; delegates of the Austro-Hungarian Government will take part in the investigations relating thereto.
7   To proceed at once to the arrest of two named men.
8   To prevent the illicit traffic in arms across the frontier.
9   To furnish explanations as to certain utterances of high Serbian officials who have expressed themselves in terms of hostility against the Austro-Hungarian Government.
10 To notify that Government, without delay, of the execution of the above measures.

The Serbian Government accepted all the above demands with the exception of demands 5 and 6. Demand 6 the Serbs rejected outright. Demand 5 they answered in such a manner as to imply rejection.

III

RESOLUTION BY GERMAN EX-SERVICE ORGANIZATIONS

On the occasion of the debate on the General Convention and the European Defence Treaty, the undersigned associations having regard to the problem of "war-criminals," have passed the following resolution on the question of a German defence contribution:

The undersigned associations note with satisfaction that Theodor Blank, the Federal Chancellor's Commissioner, has adopted their view that no German can be expected to don a military uniform again until the question of "war-criminals" has been satisfactorily settled.

Article 6 of the "Convention on the Settlement of Matters Arising out of the War and the Occupation" provides no satisfactory solution. Moreover it does not deal with the question of German soldiers detained outside the Federal Republic of Germany and of the two German soldiers detained in Spandau. Article 6, furthermore, provides for an uncertain and lengthy investigation procedure to become effective only upon the ratification of the Conventions whereby Germans become liable for military service.

The consequence of this would be that German soldiers would have to place themselves on the side of the soldiers belonging to Powers which—in violation of the spirit of the Charter on Human Rights, in particular of Articles 5 to 7— unjustly hold former German soldiers prisoner.

A German contingent formed under such circumstances within a European Army would of necessity be devoid of that soldiers' ethos which is the back-bone of every Army, and it would be exposed to the contempt of the contingents from other States. Its own nation, too, would look upon it rather as a foreign mercenary troop than as a concrete expression, arising from general conviction, of German willingness to provide a contribution to the defence of freedom.

We therefore urge a solution to the problem of "war criminals" before the formation of German contingents. A general amnesty, as a political measure, provides, in our opinion, the best possibility for an early solution to the problem. It is emphasised that crimes committed for base motives should not be included in it. Should another method be considered more practicable, there is no objection to it in so far as the problem be solved by it as quickly and thoroughly as by a general amnesty. We are thinking e.g. of the application of release on parole for all those who were of necessity convinced of the legality of their actions, coupled with the obligation to report later to the investigating committee. In appealing to the Charter on Human Rights, we urge in particular the immediate liberation of all who were sentenced by virtue of retroactive laws and of those who even to-day have not been sentenced or accused.

The decision concerning a German defence contribution is a political decision on which the political parties have different opinions. As the undersigned associations number among their members adherents to all the parties supporting our State, they do not feel competent to take a positive or negative attitude to the defence contribution.

The undersigned associations, however, expect the Federal Government and every member of the Bundestag to make the ratification of the Conventions dependent upon a solution, in the spirit of this resolution, of the problem of "war criminals":

Passed by the following Associations—representing 2 million German soldiers—listed in alphabetical order:

Federation of Emergency Associations of Former Professional Members of the Labour Service (Bund der Notgemeinschaften ehemaliger berufsmassiger Arbeitsdienstangehöriger) Bad Godesberg, Gerhard Rohlfsstr 4.

Federation of German War Wounded and Surviving Dependents (BdKK)

(Bund Deutscher Kriegsbeschädigter und Kriegshinterbliebener (BdKK)

Düsseldorf, Adersstr. 47.

The Association of Former Fighter Pilots (Gemeinschaft ehemaliger Jagdflieger) München, Schneckenburgerstr, 37 a.

Air Force Circle (Luftwaffenring) Gutersloh/Westfalen, Ostring 10.

The Traditional Association of "Greater Germany" (Traditionsgemeinschaft Grossdeutschland) Bosingfeld 394, Krs. Lemgo.

German Association of Repatriates, Prisoners-of-War and Dependents of Missing Persons (Verband der Heim-kehrer, Kriegsgefangenen und Vermissten-Angehörigen Deutschlands e.V.) Bonn, Sternstr. 63

German Association of War Wounded, Surviving Rela-tives and Social Insurance Pensioners (Verband der Kriegsbeschädigten, Kriegshinterbliebenen und Sozial-rentner Deutschlands e.V.) Bad Godesberg, Deutsch-herrenstr. 62.

Association of German Soldiers/Federation of Profes-sional Soldiers (Verband Deutscher Soldaten/Bund der Berufssoldaten) Bonn, Argelanderstr. 59

Association of Former Members of the German Afrika Corps (Verband ehemaliger Angehöriger des Deutschen Afrikakorps) Iserlohn, Gartenstr. 75

Association of Former Members of the Flying Corps (Verband ehemaliger Fliegerkorpsangehörtiger) Lübeck, Am Burgfeld 6–7.

F. D. R. der Abschrift.

(Sgd) KEILIG

Bonn, 14th July, 1952.

INDEX